Models of
Political Systems

MORTON R. DAVIES

VAUGHAN A. LEWIS

Models of

Political Systems

PRAEGER PUBLISHERS

New York · Washington · London

Published in the United States of America in 1971

Praeger Publishers, Inc.
111 Fourth Avenue, New York, N.Y. 10003, U.S.A.
5 Cromwell Place, London S.W.7, England

Printed in Great Britain

Contents

Models of Political Systems

Preface

We have incurred numerous debts of gratitude to many people. First, we would thank Professor F. F. Ridley who provided us with the original idea for such a book as this and who has continually encouraged us to reach the end of the long road to offering a completed manuscript for publication. Second, we are grateful to Richard Chapman, Anthony Beck and Robert Kilroy-Silk for reading various parts of the manuscript and offering invaluable comments. Finally, we recognize the support of our wives, who kept our lives in order while we sat and pondered universal truth. Of course, we alone are responsible for errors of fact and interpretation.

We hope that the chapters which follow will be useful to students and teachers who are wondering about the relevance and adequacy of the discipline of political science.

M.R.D.

V.A.L. January 1970

Introduction

The purpose of this study is to offer an introduction to contemporary efforts at building models to facilitate the comparative analysis of political systems in the nation-states of today. Until fairly recently, comparison was certainly not the main focus of interest in the literature of political studies. There has traditionally been a tendency to concentrate on the local scene, with only sporadic, incidental references to other political systems. The limitations and dangers of such narrow specialisms have been recognized in recent years and there is an increasing tendency to stress comparative analysis.

Persuasive reasons for such an effort lie behind this reorientation. The predominant inclination among students of politics today is to be as scientific as possible. Success in this depends on their ability to establish propositions about political behaviour whose validity transcends national boundaries. Formulating general principles concerning politics in Western democracies may be extremely difficult, but even when achieved this is quite inadequate in the heterogeneous world of the present, with its increasingly large number of diverse systems of politics which must become part of the field of inquiry of the political scientist. Politics in Communist countries and in the newly independent nations of Africa and Asia must also be taken into account. Even the most cursory of glances reveals the complexities involved in describing and analysing these vastly divergent systems with their administrative peculiarities, cultural distinctiveness and, often, their economic unpreparedness.

This desire for a scientific approach to politics has, among other reasons, led scholars to concentrate on a comparative perspective. However, recognizing the need for comparison is easier than actually coping with the problems imposed by efforts to compare on a systematic basis. This work is an attempt to describe in broad outline some of the recent responses to this need. Part One provides a historical perspective to current trends in political science; Part Two considers some of the attempts to define key concepts and to formulate hypotheses for the systematic testing of the nature of the 'political system'; and Parts Three and Four identify some of the schemas produced in recent years for actually comparing and contrasting political systems in their environments. The works discussed in Part Three concentrate on the comparison of total political systems while those considered in Part Four emphasize and differentiate the techniques and processes of power and control in society.

The following chapters are offered only as an introduction to the contemporary approach to comparative politics, and as an illustration of the type of orienting concepts used by political scientists today. They are not intended to act as a substitute for the originals, rather, it is hoped that they will encourage students to forage further into the ever-thickening jungle of model-building in political science.

MPS
$7·00

odels of
olitical Systems

orton Rees Davies and
aughan Allen Lewis

e vast amount of empirical work that has
n undertaken and the increasingly
histicated conceptual frameworks used by
temporary political scientists have
mpted many developments in the academic
dy of politics. These advances, however,
e posed a number of problems for students
s well as for lecturers and teachers—not
least of which is the dearth of suitable
ks outlining the new concepts and
ssifications. *Models of Political Systems*
vides a synopsis of some of the most
ortant recent attempts at taxonomy in the
f of political science that go beyond the
itutional framework of politics to study the
avioral and attitudinal patterns of the
erlying processes.

Part One, an introduction to the
temporary approaches to political science
ffered, as well as a brief summary of the
orical antecedents of these approaches.
s is followed by an account of a number of
mpts at identifying politics and the
litical system" and providing classificatory
emes for analyzing particular systems.
s Three and Four outline a number of
emes that classify actual political systems
rms of their over-all characteristics.

he works discussed are chosen in order
ustrate the way in which political
ntists, in developing their conceptual
eworks, have borrowed from or adapted
r disciplines. This work is not intended to
ace the original discussions of those
se works are described but to provide a
d perspective on contemporary political
nce and to encourage the pursuit of the
nces of meaning and gradations of
nction in those original works.

AUTHORS: Morton Rees Davies is
Leverhulme Lecturer in Public Administration
at the University of Liverpool, England.
Vaughan Allen Lewis is Lecturer in
Government at the University of the West
Indies, Jamaica.

CHAPTER I

The Genesis of Modern Political Theory

The kind of political theory which is described in this book—sometimes referred to as 'modern political theory' or 'modern political analysis'—has its genesis, its proponents tell us, in a general dissatisfaction with the methods of investigation into the working of the political system once characteristic mainly of British and European political scientists. In fact, we are often told,[1] there was little concern with what is now called 'the political system', but more with the study of 'the state'. And the study of the state meant analysis of the articles of constitutions (written and unwritten), legislation passed by governments, and the institutions for which the constitutions made provision. Generally when the word 'system' was used, this referred to the process of interaction between states in international relations.

The complaint was that too much emphasis came to be placed on the analysis of the law and the constitution, and that as a consequence, too little attention was given to the general social framework of the state—that is, the context within which institutions and constitutions operate. This argument was developed in the following way: societies, which are social systems, are really made up of a series of *processes*; the whole corpus of activities among men which we refer to as 'politics', and which takes place within the context of society, could also be seen as a separate and distinguishable set of processes; constitutions and institutions (parties, parliaments, bureaucracies) were in fact no more than the formalization of the more stable and recurrent of these processes.

The term 'process' was used to indicate the patterns—social or political—formed as individuals went about the necessary business of ordering the relations among themselves. The implication of this was that such patterns could be discerned by an observer, though some were more perceptible than others. Institutions, then, though they came to have a 'life' of their own, reflected something more substantial—the *structure of behaviour* of men in a variety of fields: social, political, economic—and were likely to be affected by this structure as time went on. Institutions could become outmoded: they could be seen to be failing to reflect and thus to cope with changes in the patterns or structures of behaviour among men. They then ceased to be a relevant formalization of social and other processes.

Herein lay the danger for the student of politics who concerned himself mainly with institutions or constitutions. Where these had become outmoded, or where they had been set up without sufficient regard for the social or political processes of a society, he might be studying, so to speak, the shadow rather than the substance of politics.

There was a further complaint by those who wished to foster the development of a new kind of political analysis. This was that if one attempted to analyse only the institutions and constitutions of particular countries, it became difficult to find any real basis for comparing political activity in different states. There was a tendency simply to compare the institutions of other countries by starting off with those of one's own country as the standard of comparison. And since, for example, the political institutions of Britain were often taken as among the most stable, if not *the* most stable, in the world, the procedure of political analysis usually involved taking British political institutions as the standard of comparison. There were, in fact, it was argued, no objective criteria provided for comparison; thus there was not a satisfactory basis for the *comparative study of politics.*

A further practical point was involved here. It was claimed that when it became necessary to set up political institutions in other countries—especially in colonial countries—constitutional advisors (who happened often to be academic students of politics) were inclined to suggest institutions which were essentially similar to those existing in Britain or other metropolitan countries, rather than to recommend the setting up of institutions which took account of and, in part, reflected the patterns of social and political behaviour in the particular territories. The proponents of a modern political theory, on the other hand, tended to point out, if sometimes only by implication, that whereas in the United States the political institutions had been set up by the inhabitants of the territory themselves, and not by metropolitan *diktat*, these institutions were substantially different from, and almost incapable of comparison with, those existing in the United Kingdom; even though care had been taken to institutionalize certain *ideas* about how political activity ought to be undertaken, common to both countries. It was possible to compare the extent to which different kinds of institutions coped with the problems common to political activity everywhere (for example, the elementary one of the preservation of order) and to compare how these institutions allowed for behaviour necessary for 'proper' political activity (for example, freedom of speech and equal treatment by government of all individuals) but not to compare the institutions themselves, since these were not similar to each other.

We are not concerned to discuss the validity of these complaints, but to point out that they were the sources of dissatisfaction with the existing study of politics and that they provided an impetus to the search for a new 'science' of politics: new methods and theories to explain and compare political activity and arrangements in a variety of countries. And an important assumption here was that, although certain functions had to be performed in all countries if there was to be political activity at all, social arrangements often differed from country to country, and since social arrangements were likely to condition the kinds of political institutions that developed, political institutions—the mechanisms for performing political functions—were likely to differ from country to country. Political institutions, in other words, were partially *derivative* from social arrangements, though they could, in turn, be used to change social arrangements. The mechanisms of politics (which are all that institutions and constitutions are) perform certain functions which are necessary for the maintenance of government in all types of countries. To compare political activity in various countries it was possible to compare mechanisms in terms of their performance of these functions which are *objective* requirements of all political activity.

The search for a new political science, with its emphasis on the structure and functions of political behaviour, really came into prominence after the Second World War. As we have already hinted, the impetus for it involved both theoretical and practical considerations. Four of these seem to us particularly important:

1. It became necessary to attempt to explain in some objective manner the failure of 'democracy' and the rise of authoritarian political institutions in Germany during the inter-war period. Germany had been looked upon as a state similar enough in economic and social development to, for example, Britain and it had been assumed that the operation of the Weimar constitution would lead to that stable political activity characteristic of the Western liberal democracies.* Coupled with this was some dismay at the unorthodox kinds of political activity that characterized certain of the new states created in Central Europe after the First World War.

2. With the creation of new states after the Second World War, first in Asia and then in Africa, political scientists found

* The Weimar constitution followed, in the main, French practice. But the important point for us is that its failure led to a deepening concern with the relation between constitutions and social circumstances; and among American political scientists, some of whom were of German extraction, there developed a concern with the social basis of the political activity that led to the rise of the Nazis.

themselves presented with new opportunities to study, for theoretical and practical purposes, what was sometimes called 'the social conditions of democracy'. The failure of the 'colonial' constitutions in some of these countries gave an additional impetus to this.

3. In pursuit of the scientific study of politics it was felt necessary to develop a theoretical analysis of politics which explained the genesis of different kinds of political institutions. The only claimant to this was Marxist political theory which, its critics argued, was not scientific. Some non-Marxist theory was necessary which linked social and political processes and which was capable of explaining the origins, development and capacity for change of political systems. A theory of this type would, by definition, be *predictive* and thus further the unity of 'the theory and practice' of politics. There was, then, a desire to pattern the science of politics on the methods of investigation of the natural sciences.

4. If, as suggested in point 3, a scientific study was possible then a truly comparative study of politics would also become possible. With the great increase in the number of independent states with social structures different from those characteristic of Western countries, a theory of comparative political processes was deemed, more than ever, necessary.

It would be misleading to suggest that, in attempting to devise a theory or theories of political behaviour that link other social processes to those of politics, modern political theorists are claiming to be the first to attempt this. Though they would no doubt claim to be systematizing the study of politics in a new way, by, for example, deriving concepts that do not have overt ethical implications likely to prejudice analysis (following Max Weber's injunctions on the 'ethically neutral' or 'value free' nature of scientific analysis), by devising methods for extensive investigation of the empirical basis of political activity, and by stating the results of their analysis in such a way that the results are open to verification or disproval, these theorists recognize some early, if unsystematic, progenitors. We have already mentioned Karl Marx, sometimes given a somewhat hesitant recognition.[2] There is also the old tradition combining classification of political regimes with discussion of the kinds of regimes that 'fit' particular social conditions, stemming from Aristotle and including de Tocqueville's analysis of *Democracy in America*.[3]

Here we might also take note of the work of another nineteenth-century figure, the Frenchman Auguste Comte, who is reputed to have coined the word 'sociology'. He was concerned with developing a science of social relations and in doing so devoted much attention to discussing the extent to which the form of society and the stages of its development determined the character of the state that came into being and the various political institutions of the state. Comte, in fact, subordinated the state to something, but in so far as he tried to suggest that social structure had, to put it at its lowest, a major influence on state formation and development, he pointed the way to a comparative sociology of politics. For Comte, as for Marx, the importance of a scientific understanding of society lies in the implications of this understanding for changing and controlling society. Comte did have a certain influence in South America and, with his compatriot Saint Simon, in the French colonies. He has not, however, had a major influence on contemporary sociologists or political theorists.[4] Comte's counterpart in England and, in the view of some, more important because his influence extended to the United States, was Herbert Spencer. Spencer, attracted to the writings of Darwin, tried to suggest that there were certain processes common to the development and survival of living things and that of social structures.

But among the students of politics whose work during and towards the end of the nineteenth century helped to pinpoint the difficulties of linking the analysis of social structure with that of political behaviour, and are therefore of some relevance, were two Englishmen, Walter Bagehot and Graham Wallas.*

* Unlike Comte and Marx, however, Bagehot and Wallas were fundamentally interested in *political* behaviour and not simply in the implications

Bagehot, in his series of articles collected under the title, *The English Constitution*, written in 1865 and 1866, attempted to show how the social conditions of England at that time influenced the political institutions that had been devised; how these institutions were themselves, in part, a cloak, hiding much more substantial political activity; how the 'unseen' political process, which could not be analysed in terms of the stated purposes of the political institutions, contributed to maintaining the political and social stability. To this Bagehot added a psychological analysis of the various classes of individuals in England.

But even Bagehot, by the time he came to write an introduction to the second edition of *The English Constitution*, found himself up against a problem with which modern political theory still attempts to grapple: how, if one is to go beyond the study of mere institutions, are processes—continually changing relationships—to be depicted, and yet be made to seem more than merely a snapshot of a political system at one particular period of time? 'There is,' Bagehot wrote in 1872, 'a great difficulty in the way of a writer who attempts to sketch a living constitution—a Constitution that is in actual work and power. The difficulty is that the object is in constant change . . . The difficulty is the greater because a writer who deals with a living government naturally compares it with the most important other living governments, and these are changing too, what he illustrates are altered probably in one way, and his sources of illustration are altered probably in a different way.' It is, in passing, interesting to compare this observation with one made somewhat more dramatically by Marx in 1867: '. . . within the ruling classes themselves a foreboding is dawning, that the present society is no solid crystal, but an organism capable of change, and is constantly changing'.[5]

Graham Wallas, in his *Human Nature in Politics*, published in 1908, laid further stress on what we can call the socio-

---

of social structure for politics or in the general analysis of social structures and relations.

psychological foundations of political behaviour. Individuals were not, in their reaction to social and political events, as rational as the men of the Enlightenment might have inclined us to think. Often men thought in terms of images (a cluster of ideas about, for example, a political party) which remained with, and had an influence upon them long after the sources of these images had themselves changed. Of 'the facts of human nature,' he wrote, 'deliberate thought is only one,' and he deplored the tendency during his age of political analysis to neglect the many facets of man's nature and the influences of these upon the political attitudes he held and the choices which he made. 'The student of politics must, consciously or unconsciously, form a conception of human nature, and the less conscious he is of his conception the more likely he is to be dominated by it.'[6] Modern political theory has attempted to refine this strand of Wallas' thinking.[7]

From another, somewhat different, tradition, another of the major influences on the new approach to political theory has been the work of the German Max Weber (1864–1920). His descriptions and analyses of different types of social action have been refined by Talcott Parsons who, now perhaps the most famous American sociologist, has attempted to devise a coherent and general theory of social relations, including political relations. Weber's development of the 'ideal type'[8] as a methodological device for describing and explaining different kinds of systems has been found useful by some theorists, though it has been subjected to criticism;[9] we have already mentioned the political scientists' attachment to Weber's suggestion that analysis be, to the extent that this is possible, 'ethically neutral' or 'value free'. Talcott Parsons, who has been much influenced by Weber has, in turn, with the development of his 'structural-functional' model been much drawn on by some of the writers whom we consider in this book.[10]

Finally, it is important to note, in discussing the predecessors of present-day modern political theorists, that there has been in the United States what we shall call a tradition of 'scientific politics'. This has been referred to and discussed by an English student of politics, Bernard Crick, as *The American Science of Politics*. Crick, though critical of this tradition, attempts to show that the intellectual ground in the United States has been more favourable than that of England, for example, to the encouragement of the growth of the idea that social science should be made as systematic as possible, following the pattern of the natural sciences.

We can briefly examine this tradition both in terms of its own indigenous development and in terms of influences from some of the sociological thinkers to whom we have referred above. The indigenous aspect lies, as we have earlier suggested, in the concern with political *behaviour*. The very discussion relating to the formation of a constitution for the United States concerned itself with the attempt to derive a variable balance between the varieties of groups and 'social forces' existing in that country. The federalist constitution was seen, therefore, to use modern phraseology, as a mechanism of social and political control, but one that was to prove reasonably successful, not because it allowed any one group to attain predominant political power, but because it made provision for groups in (political) interaction to check each other, so that no absolute predominance could be established.

It is this 'practical' background that forms the basis of the concern with what came to be called a 'group theory of politics'. The works of Bentley and Truman,[11] which can be taken as indicative of the development of the field, constituted attempts to systematize knowledge about the 'pluralist' nature of the politics of that society. This approach has been pursued by a number of authors.

To a concern for relations between groups and between groups and political institutions was added a slightly different, though not unrelated, dimension: the attempt to analyse the importance of 'power in society'. It can hardly be claimed that the study of power constitutes a new field for students of politics, but what was here attempted, predominantly by Harold Lasswell and his associates,[12] was an application of the psychological approach, so that the motives of men concerned with the acquisition and use of power and the reactions of those who subordinated themselves to such power could be incorporated in the analysis. The aim was therefore to make systematic knowledge about power and other concepts usually associated with it—influence, control and so on. These two lines of development have been further developed and, to some extent, united by, for example, Dahl.[13]

The major external sociological influence, and a fairly extensive one, on contemporary American writing has been, as we have hinted, the work of Max Weber, introduced chiefly through the explications and translations of Talcott Parsons. Weber's work has spawned a literature that attempts to link sociological analysis to political behaviour, stretching from what has been called 'historical sociology' to the study of the relations between individuals, groups and structures in organizations both governmental and non-governmental.

CHAPTER II

The Nature of Modern Political Analysis

THEORY AND METHODOLOGY

From the traditions mentioned above stems a variety of methodological approaches in modern political science (which, we might observe, now becomes essentially political science as developed in the United States). The underlying assumptions of these approaches we will briefly note.

First, the distinction was made between 'theory' and 'ideology', or to put this in another way, between scientific theorizing and that theorizing, characteristic of the 'masters of political thought', which sought to suggest what were the 'right' forms of political organization and sets of relationships within which men might acquire a maximum degree of liberty. These were now referred to as 'doctrine', having in the main a normative character. For modern political scientists these doctrines or philosophies, though sometimes severely analytical, were not sufficiently grounded in empirical fact.[1]

Secondly, while the emphasis of the Oxford School on the importance of logic in the making of political statements[2] was accepted as relevant, there was the suggestion that this approach did not constitute a satisfying one; it was a useful part, but would not form the basis, since it placed little importance on the description and analysis of behaviour, or empirical political theory.

Finally, there was the assumption that if the study of political behaviour was to be made scientific—subject to the discovery of laws—then mathematical and statistical analysis was a useful tool of investigation. This took two main directions. First, there was the introduction of statistical methods into the study of the relation between electoral behaviour and social structure—thus, for example, the utility and consequent development of public opinion polling. Second, there developed the view that if models of political behaviour were to be devised, then it might be possible to suggest logical (and by implication, mathematical) relationships between the variables in these models. This is implicit in many of the models developed by the analysts whom we shall consider in this book, and is made quite explicit in the work of, for example, Karl Deutsch.

We can note, however, that this emphasis on mathematical models could be, and was subsequently, utilized as a means of further developing the approach to political analysis which concerned itself with concepts such as power and influence and the relationships within and between groups involved in political interaction.[3] What came to be called 'small groups behaviour' now constituted an important subject of study, and was applied to, for example, the study of political coalitions within and between states.

THEORY AND SYSTEM

But the most recent and fundamental idea which modern political scientists claim to have introduced into the study of politics in the effort to make a more systematic discipline is that, as we have hinted above, political life should be seen as a 'system' or a set of systems of interaction. From here the notion develops that political analysis is no more than a form of 'systems analysis'.

The concept of system is one borrowed from the natural sciences, and difficulties arise when it is adopted for the analysis of social and political phenomena. In the natural sciences the system concept is usually used to refer to fairly clearly defined sets of interactions, around which recognizable boundaries can be drawn. The sets of interactions which constitute the political system, however, cannot be so completely or clearly isolated, and the operation of the system is influenced very considerably not only by the interactions which are internal to itself, but also by interactions which fall outside its boundaries.

Thus the political scientist wishing to use the concept of system is faced with the difficulty not only of determining which interactions properly constitute the political system, but also of developing conceptual tools capable of indicating the exchanges between a political system and its environment. To account for what happens in a political system solely in terms of its internal activities, isolated from the influences of its environment, involves a superficial view of political life as a *closed* system. To be of use to the political scientist therefore the system concept must be capable of incorporating the part played by the non-political aspects of social life. Thus the political system must be seen as an *open* system—that is, it is open to outside influences.

We shall discuss this in detail later, for it is held to be the key concept of modern political science. Almond suggests that its introduction is to be seen as a vital step in the development of a science of politics. It provides an orienting concept that is likely to promote political enquiry along new and fruitful avenues in a manner similar to that in which Enlightenment political theory carried political studies beyond that facilitated by earlier classical theories. It can also, in his view, be compared to the major developments of American empirical theory in the first half of this century.[4] Further, it is a concept which can be used to interpret political activity wherever this may occur, and not simply at the level of national politics—the level of the state. Whatever the differences between national and international politics, for example, it is held that in both fields the concept of system can be used as the starting point of analysis.

To the more traditional students of politics this is a large claim. It goes against the belief, still strongly held, that the phenomena and their manner of behaviour in international relations are different from their counterparts in domestic politics, thus the two fields cannot be analysed with the aid of the same concepts.[5] Modern political science or systems analysis, on the other hand, now claims to be able to ignore these traditional sub-divisions of political analysis.

Differences of this nature with respect to, in particular, the analysis of national and international politics reflect, one finds, differences in attitudes to the nature of political analysis as a whole; that is to say, differences in beliefs about the extent to which various sectors of political life are susceptible to what may be called scientific theorizing. It is useful, therefore, to describe now some of the ideas on methodology which are characteristic of modern political science.

The aim of modern political scientists is the creation of *systematic theory*. In this connection, Easton, among others, writing in 1953 complained that there had been a dearth of orienting concepts in political science in recent decades, this resulting in what he called 'hyperfactualism'—that is, too much concentration on gathering facts, and too little attention being given to the promulgation of theories capable of explaining their significance.[6] Clearly, he was not thinking of theory in the sense that we use the phrase when we refer to the political theory of Hobbes or Bentham. The word theory itself has obviously many meanings even among those solely concerned with political analysis. Easton is concerned with what he calls 'causal theory' which 'seeks to show the relation among political facts'. The very existence of such theory, he believes, is an indication of the development of any science, both social and physical, and a necessary prerequisite to the attainment of reliable knowledge.[7] That he wishes to emulate the method of the natural sciences is clear. He wishes to devise a method for ordering the various phenomena of political life, so that knowledge gained about one sphere of politics and the concepts derived for interpreting this sphere, can be used in trying to understand other spheres and even in predicting what may happen in all spheres in the future.

Other practitioners of modern political science are in agreement with him here. Theoretical knowledge in this sense is assumed, as it is in the natural sciences, to be *cumulative*. And a major assumption about the development of cumulative knowledge with respect to politics (as in other fields) is that the various facets of political life are all related to each other. This assumption has, as we shall see, a direct relation to the decision to describe political life as 'a system'; for in the natural sciences at least, a system is made of interrelated parts—parts connected in some way to each other and dependent upon each other for their existence.

Since there is a connection being made between social science analysis and natural science analysis, let us take a definition of theory from a philosopher of natural science. Norwood Hanson asks, 'What is it to supply a theory?' He goes on to suggest that 'it is *at least* this: to offer an intelligible, systematic, conceptual pattern for the observed data. The value of such a pattern lies in its capacity to unite phenomena which, without the theory, are either surprising, anomalous, or left wholly unnoticed.'[8] A theory then is not simply a description; it is an analytical device (a set of principles), a 'conceptual pattern' which, at a minimum assists in, and at best is a prerequisite to, explaining and predicting phenomena.

Now though we are not concerned to arbitrate between them, we must indicate that it is on the question of whether the phenomena of politics can be, as a whole, systematized—that is, can be subsumed under a general theory—that traditional analysts contest the claims of the modernists. Further, the traditionalists wonder whether what they see as very diverse phenomena, involving the activity of human beings, can be made the subject of prediction or even of theories designed to specify the properties of political systems in such a way that they might prove themselves capable of analysis and characterization in mathematical and statistical terms.[9] For with respect to the natural sciences, and even in some of the social sciences (such as economics), 'To propose something as a theory of (an) x . . . is to suggest that x's are governed by such and such principles, not just that it is useful for certain purposes to represent *x's* as governed by these principles or that such principles approximate those which actually obtain. Accordingly, the scientists who propose something as a theory of (an) *x* must hold that alternative theories are to be rejected, or modified, or understood as holding only for special cases, or something of the like.'[10] It is, perhaps, this definitiveness of explanation of a set of phenomena, required by a scientific theory, that goes most against the grain for traditionalists.

To assume that one can provide a theory explaining a set of occurrences involves assuming that these occurrences are characterized by certain *laws* of behaviour; and to say that laws can be discerned is another way of saying that the phenomena under observation recur in a similar fashion sufficiently often as to be made the subject of remarks of the following kind: ' on the basis of our observation of a number of phenomena called *x*, we can predict that if *x* occur again in a certain context (under similar conditions) then the behaviour of *x* will have the consequence or consequences *y*'; or 'on the basis of our observation of the behaviour of a number (*n*) of people in a given situation, in the future, other things remaining the same, the majority of these *n* people are likely to behave in a certain manner, *m*'. A prediction of the second kind—specifying a *probability* that certain things are likely to happen—is the type involved in, for example, studies of the electoral process.

Modern political scientists aim at making law-like statements of this kind. And as a prerequisite to doing this, they assume that the political phenomena which they observe are sufficiently recurrent and similar (if not exactly the same) in their recurrence, to be the subject of law-like statements.

Now, if one can discern laws in the behaviour of individuals, in the behaviour of groups of individuals, or in the behaviour of institutions constituted by individuals, then it is possible to create *models* of such behaviour or activity. To put this more specifically, if the individuals who vote for political parties, the political parties themselves, or even the government of a state can be seen to act over some period of time consistently, in particular ways, then it becomes possible to devise models of such individual or institutional activity. It becomes possible to create a variety of models of activity within and of the political system, and then, perhaps, to create a *theory* of the political system as a whole. There can be alternative (different) models of the working of an institution (a party or a state) depending on the particular problem with which one is concerned with respect to that institution, but there can only be *one theory* of the behaviour of that institution, for a theory takes into account the various models of institutional behaviour that can be devised, and thus may be able to account—to provide an explanation—for all possible forms of the behaviour of the institution.

A model need only account for some particular aspect[11] of the behaviour of an institution. In this sense, a theory gives a deeper (or, perhaps better, a more over-arching) explanation of behaviour than a model. But it may not always be possible to formulate a theory, whereas it may be possible to devise models of certain activities with the information at hand. A model, which, clearly, may consist of certain theoretical assumptions, is devised for the purpose of attempting to construct an empirical theory of the behaviour of some entity. A model, therefore, while not a replica or description of the entity under observation must contain a representation of the main features of the entity; the description given by a model must approximate the entity with whose behaviour the analyst is concerned. It can thus provide the empirical basis for the theory to be devised—since a theory is no more than a set of principles. Where the model is used to provide the verification or disproof of a suggested theory then one is involved in the foundation of that 'empirical theory' to which Easton refers and which modern political scientists assert as their aim. We can perhaps see now that the construction of, at least, models (assuming that this is possible with respect to political phenomena) might be of some assistance in attempting to cope with Bagehot's problem (referred to above) of explaining the workings of a 'living constitution', an 'object [that] is in constant change'.

The problem for modern political scientists is how to set about creating models of political activity in its various forms: models for the explanation of men, each a 'unique' being in social and political interaction dealing with problems and in circumstances which, from day to day, are never exactly the same again. This last statement, perhaps, exaggerates the difficulties involved; for though situations differ in detail from day to day, certain political situations, for example, elections, are recognized as being sufficiently *alike*, to be susceptible of characterization under one heading, to be given the same name. In other words we are able to abstract from certain situations and to describe them in terms of the same *concept*. A concept, then, is a term used to 'class' a set of objects which we recognize as being reasonably similar in appearance and behaviour. It is a form of shorthand which gives us an initial indication that certain activities are of a type with which we are already familiar. Thus if we use concepts such as 'election' or 'party' we may recognize in a number of other countries certain activities and relations between individuals with which we are associated in our own country.

And the utility of a concept lies precisely in the degree to which the activities that it connotes are recognized as being 'reasonably similar'. If the 'class' of objects to which the concept refers comes to be recognized, when investigated, as containing components and patterns of behaviour which are very dissimilar, then the concept which we have been using loses its usefulness as an analytical or investigatory tool.

CONCEPTS OF MODERN POLITICAL SCIENCE

The claim of modern political scientists is that they have, first of all, suggested a new set of concepts for political analysis, as the first step towards the construction of models and theories of the political process. We have already referred to their disdain of the concept of 'the state' as an analytical tool. Instead, one

writer has suggested that to find appropriate conceptual categories for the comparison of political systems which are fundamentally different in terms of size, structure and culture, the
modernists have had to borrow extensively from sociological
and anthropological theory. Among the more important of the
borrowed concepts are: political system, role, political culture,
political structure and political socialization.[12]

The key concept, as we suggested above, is that of *system*, and
we shall be concerned with discussing it during the rest of this
chapter. For the most easily available definition of this concept,
we can take first that given in the *Concise Oxford Dictionary* where
we find: 'System: 1. Complex whole, set of connected things or
parts, organized body of material or immaterial things . . . 2.
Method, organization, considered principles of procedure,
(principle of) classification . . .'. The significant words here are
obviously 'connected', 'organized', 'organization'. That a
system must be organized or have organization, that its parts
must be connected—these properties are necessary to anything
defined as a system. We might note also that these properties are
recognized by natural scientists when dealing with phenomena
in their fields. A biologist, Ludwig Bertallanfy has, for example,
written that, 'Every organism represents *a system* by which term
we mean a complex of elements in mutual interaction'; in an
organism 'each part and each individual event depends not only
on conditions within itself, but also to a greater or lesser extent
on conditions within the *whole*, or within superordinate units of
which it is a part . . . The problem of life is that of organization.' [13]

It is scarcely necessary to observe that it is from this kind of
conception that social scientists have, in recent years, derived
their own definitions. On the whole, they have tended to accept,
as defining characteristics of social systems, those of living
systems: integration, regularity, wholeness, organization, coherence, connectedness or interdependence of parts. It is further
assumed that a system must 'maintain' its identity over some
period of time if it is to be characterized as such.

Modern political scientists or systems analysts have assumed that *political* systems (we shall see below how these are defined), like all other systems, approximate to these characteristics. Almond, for example, sees in the use of legitimate force the particular quality which transcends all the aspects of political life, thus identifying the political as a separate body of activity and the aspect which gives that activity its systemic coherence. Other properties which the interactions of a political system possess are identified by him as comprehensiveness, interdependence and the existence of boundaries.[14]

Similarly Easton identifies a number of the defining characteristics of living systems as premises for a meaningful use of the concept of system in political science. For example, he identifies political life as a system of behaviour, distinguishable from the environment within which it exists, but open to influences from that environment. He views changes in the structures and processes of the system as the results of efforts to cope with stress as it arises, thus showing the capacity of the system to maintain its identity over a period of time. Finally, such a system is characterized by a capacity for 'feedback', thus allowing it to 'persist' in the face of environmental stress. By a feedback capacity is meant the possession of mechanisms which can absorb, and transmit to the system, information from its environment relevant to its continuing existence and activity.[15]

Whatever the differences between proponents of systems analysis, the idea that political life, and thus the societies of which they are part, are 'coherent' systems with interdependent parts is common to them all. We must observe, however, that some philosophers demur from this emphasis on coherence and interdependence. 'A society,' one has written, 'is a *process* with *some* systematic characteristics, rather than a closely integrated system, like an organism or a machine.'[16]

It is important to emphasize, however, that when modern political scientists use the concept 'system', it is used as an *analytical* concept and not necessarily to describe or reflect a *concrete* system, for the interactions which interest political scientists form only a part of the total interactions of a society. The concept of system is used by political scientists to identify and analyse that part of this totality which falls within their sphere of interest.

This totality of interactions is a *concrete* system, conceptualized as a coherent body of activities with *definite* boundaries and clearly identifiable as a reflection of some real social entity. Talcott Parsons, in fact, argues that the *only* concrete type system is the *total* set of social interactions. His structural-functional model of the social system is an attempt to represent this reality. The basic entity for analysis is the entire social system whose main function is identified as the survival or self-maintenance of that society. Such a comprehensive model is, however, too unwieldy to be operationalized meaningfully *as a whole* by empirical social scientists.

Consequently this model of the social system and the basic notion of function are both subdivided into a series of subsystem functions which largely correspond to conventional classifications of social behaviour, and which, in the main, are divided according to the subject matters of the 'conventional' disciplines within the social sciences. These subsystems are therefore abstracted or *analytic* systems, the boundaries of which do not have to be physically defined, nor, for example, have a geographical correspondence; they refer to sets of interactions which have been abstracted from the whole body of social behaviour within which they occur.[17] We shall enlarge on this point when we discuss the particular authors with whom we are concerned in this book.

But the preceding discussion will have intimated that concepts other than those already mentioned in the quotation from Almond follow from the use of the concept of system. Systems are deemed to consist of 'subsystems', 'boundaries', 'environments'.

A subsystem is simply a system which may be discerned to form part of some larger system or whole. Though it may have an existence of its own, and can in investigation be treated as a separate entity, it is dependent for its activity or viability on the larger system, regardless of its importance for the existence and activity of that system.

The concept of a boundary refers to the points at which, in analytical terms, other systems end and the political system begins. The boundary between society and polity is not fixed or constant: it differs from political system to political system and may, with respect to any one political system, alter considerably over a period of time. Clearly, this emphasizes the point that we have already made, that when we speak of a boundary, the term is not used to refer to some concrete line in a geographical sense. A boundary which a political scientist posits as existing between a political system which he has abstracted from 'society', or between a political system and an economic or cultural system is an analytic one; it is made, so to speak, in the mind of the observer, partly for his own convenience for analysing a particular problem which he has chosen.

This leads us to the notion of environment. The environment of an object is constituted by anything that surrounds that object. A political system exists in the general environment of society. Society is itself constituted of a number of systems besides the political: for example, economic and cultural systems, as well as, of course, biological systems—men. If a political system is defined, as systems analysts define it, as an *open* system, one that is subject to penetration by and the influence of, other systems, then these latter systems will leave some mark on the operation of the political system and on those who participate in its operation. So, in a real or concrete political system (for example, the state) individuals are subject to, and even conditioned by, the particular cultural system of the society into which they are born. And it is possible to analyse the extent to which the culture of society, which includes rules on how to engage in political and social activity, is adopted by those who participate in the working of the political system: the extent to which they become politically socialized.[18]

Finally, since individuals in society take part in a number of systems and subsystems, they are in fact acting in different capacities as they engage in one type of behaviour and then another in 'moving' from system to system. That is to say, they adopt different *roles* in the variety of systems in which they concern themselves. Systems analysis is concerned, then not so much with individuals as such, but rather with the roles that individuals play and their interactions. Since the concept of role is really transferred by analogy from the world of the theatre, and it is obvious that an actor does not necessarily have to believe in the validity or adopt the beliefs characteristic of the role which he is playing, we can see that the systems analyst is concerned not so much with the personal attitudes of the individual who is a politician or participating in the political process by, for example, voting. He is really concerned to analyse either the extent to which the individual may be affected by these attitudes when he has assumed (is playing) a particular role, or the extent to which an individual believes that the adoption of an attitude is instrumental to the 'proper' playing of a role. The political scientist analyses the structure of a system with roles as variables of analysis of that structure. The concept of role is another analytic concept.

We shall describe how these concepts, and others which flow from them, are used and extended by a number of political scientists in their attempt to develop methods of explaining and comparing the workings and development of the variety of political entities which exist in the world today.

PART TWO

Structural-Functional Analysis,
General Systems Theory,
Communications Theory

CHAPTER III

Introduction

'The proper business of any scientist,' a logician has written, 'is not to study a "subject" but to study actual problems.'[1] If there is a problem about the behaviour of some aspect of political phenomena that intrigues us, then we attempt to perceive the reasons for the particular form of behaviour. And 'as soon as we enquire into the *reasons* for the [behaviour of] the phenomena, we enter the domain of theory . . .'[2] It must be remembered, then, that the purpose of theory building, the suggestion of hypotheses or the construction of models in any science, social or natural, is precisely to assist us in the explanation or solution of particular problems: to aid in perceiving the connection between phenomena and the behaviour which they exhibit. Scientific investigation is not concerned simply with describing and naming (that is, with finding new *concepts*), nor with taxonomy or classification, though these constitute a part of the enterprise.

It is important to emphasize this, for one of the complaints made about contemporary political science has been that it has been concerned perhaps excessively with concept formation (i.e. giving new names to political activities) and with classification of types of behaviour and institutions, and not sufficiently with explanations of political phenomena and the problems associated with them.

It is in the light of these observations that the success or failure of the works which we describe in this book must be judged. And though we are not here concerned with 'judging', in our description of selected writers' works, we are concerned with, first, the problems which they think need to be explained; then with the theories and methods which they have devised; and finally with how far they estimate that these theories and methods are apposite to the solution of the problems which they have perceived: in other words, to what extent they succeed, even in their own estimation, in achieving 'empirical theory'.

Again, however, as we have seen, political scientists have been concerned not simply with solving observable political problems, but with a range of activities which they perceive as important to undertake before engaging in explanation and solution of the problems. They have continued to discuss extensively the 'status' of their subject: that is the extent to which political problems are in fact capable of being analysed in scientific terms at all—whether politics is really a 'science' as they conceive science. A consequence of this is that there is much discussion of methodology: of *how* the study of political phenomena ought to be approached. Modern political scientists claim that the discipline as they conceive it is a new one, and that this stage of the discussion of methodology—involving, for example, discussing whether the discipline ought to be eclectic in terms of other existing sciences—is a necessary one in its development.[3]

CHAPTER IV

G. A. Almond's Analysis

The problems with which Almond and his associates are concerned are two which are interlinked. First they wish to construct a theory (or perhaps, at present, an approach to a theory) which will explain how political systems change in type from, to use the current phraseology, the 'traditional' to the 'modern'. This is of interest because they assume that modern systems are more 'efficient' in coping with the political problems in a state as, in particular, it moves from the lower (predominantly non-mechanized agricultural) to more developed (predominantly industrial) stages of economic development and with the social arrangements that go with these stages. To put this in a few words, they wish to devise a 'theory of political development'. We shall return to this.

But second, Almond (we shall from here on use Almond's name to refer to himself and those with whom he has collaborated) is also concerned to classify, in some meaningful way, the different types of political systems and regimes that may exist. This is, as we have seen, an exercise in typology construction. Implicit in the arrangement of systems by type are evaluations about the manner in which the systems differ in terms of their efficiency. It thus becomes possible to arrange political systems in terms of a scale: if it is assumed that certain tasks must be performed by a political system in a particular social and economic condition, then it is possible to say that certain systems perform these tasks more efficiently than others *in the same condition*. This is not to assert, as Almond points out, that 'one *class* of political system is better than another'.[1] But he argues that if one sets out to develop a 'science of comparative politics', then a first task must be that of describing with some accuracy, and then classifying, the political processes that occur in a variety of societies, according to a common set of criteria.[2]

It is when these two problems to which we refer are satisfactorily dealt with, that comparison becomes possible.

To return to the first problem, it is necessary first to examine a few elementary terms used by Almond. Let us note that there is an assumption that political *change* can be seen in terms of *development*. Such an assumption further implies that it is possible to show, in some way, the end product, or at least *an* end product, of this development and that it may be possible to divide the development process into a number of stages. Thus Almond refers to countries as being, broadly, either 'traditional', 'transitional' or 'modern'. 'There is', he has written, 'a logic to the process of development', so that it is possible 'to explain and even predict cycles of short-range and long-range change [of the political system] in response to various kinds of environmental pressures.' [3] It might be claimed that these terms imply a form of teleological analysis, but Almond might reply, while admitting this, that he would not claim, as the Greek political theorists would have, that he can foresee or posit the *final* end or state of the developmental process. Thus, though the analysis may be teleological,[4] that is, it may seem to suggest that the processes being analysed will inevitably arrive at some end-point or final state, the important thing is that development is, for him, an open-ended process.

One can, however, see that the use of these terms implies an analysis somewhat similar to that of 'living things', organisms,[5] which has come down to political scientists not simply through, for example, students interested in biological analysis such as Aristotle, but in more modern times through some of the proponents of modern sociology. Almond in fact has been concerned, particularly in the work which he has done since his 'Introduction' to his *The Politics of the Developing Areas*, to show the difference between his kind of developmental analysis and that characteristic of both the Aristotelians and modern sociologists, while, however, clearly claiming that he has been influenced by and drawn on sociological and anthropological analysis and that his approach therefore is indeed an eclectic one. One can easily see why; for it is one of his further assumptions that 'political systems are a class' of social systems,[6] and although he believes that political systems have distinct characteristics of their own, he acknowledges that the concepts and perceptions of other disciplines in general, and other social sciences in particular, are instrumental in gaining an understanding of politics.

We might note in passing, since the study of new nations has attracted as many economists as political scientists, that developmental and 'stages' analysis has also become familiar in the study of economic development.[7]

If one is analysing political systems in terms of levels of development, there must be some particular point of comparison, in default of some other objective one. Almond's procedure was to identify the functions of the polity in modern Western systems, and then to pursue his analysis of political modernization in non-Western areas by investigating how these functions, which are associated with distinctive political activities in Western systems, are performed elsewhere. The basis for this view is Almond's own belief that anyone who wishes to understand the process of modernization in non-Western societies must first be capable of understanding the processes of development and current behaviour of the societies which, he claims, can be called 'modern', that is, Western societies.[8]

It remains finally to look at Almond's particular definition of 'political system'. What he attempts to do is to amend and enlarge Max Weber's definition, which emphasized the notion of dominance of a particular territory as germane to any identification of a political system which then becomes the same as a 'state'. Second, he wishes to stress that the purpose of politics is not simply that of achieving social integration, but that the political system has as one of its main aspects the preservation of order, which may be anterior to social integration. Thus the political system 'is that system of interaction to be found in all independent societies which performs the functions of integration and adaptation (both internationally and *vis-à-vis* other societies) by means of the employment or threat of employment, of more or less legitimate physical compulsion. The political system is the legitimate, order-maintaining or transforming system in the society . . . legitimate force is the thread that runs through the inputs and outputs of the political system, giving it its special quality and salience and its coherence as a system'.[9]

Structural-functional analysis is then, a form of *systemic analysis* which looks at political systems as coherent wholes which influence and are in turn influenced by their environments,[10] and for Almond it is the presence of 'legitimate force' throughout the system—in the last analysis holding it together—that allows one to look at it in scientific terms; that is, as a 'whole'. Political systems therefore can be characterized by *comprehensiveness, interdependence,* and the *existence of boundaries.* Furthermore, the interactions which characterize political systems (as particular kinds of social systems) take place between, not individuals, but the roles individuals adopt: these are the basic units of structural-functional analysis. Finally, political systems are *open systems,* that is, they are engaged in communicating with entities and systems beyond their own boundaries, and they are affected by and react to what happens beyond those boundaries in their environment.

THE METHOD OF ANALYSIS

Structural-functional analysis can be said to have originated in the biological and mechanical sciences. Within the social sciences it was first used in anthropology, but was later developed and refined as a mode of sociological analysis, predominantly by Talcott Parsons and Marion Levy.[11] For these theorists the basic assumptions of this analysis are that all systems have structures which can be identified and that the parts or elements of these structures perform functions within the system which have meaning only in terms of the working of the system. They are dependent on the system as an active entity for their existence, and are, in turn, linked in such a way as to be also dependent on each other for their activity. Systems cannot be defined as such if their constituent parts are not *functionally interdependent*, and these parts can only be understood as performing functions if they belong to a complete system. Further, systems, defined in this way are held to have a tendency towards equilibrium and Parsons has himself asserted that the theory of social control 'like the theory of deviance . . . must always be stated relative to a given state of equilibrium of the system or subsystem'.[12]

The term, equilibrium, has been subjected to much critical analysis. Easton[13] has described the different concepts of equilibrium that have appeared. In the most general sense, equilibrium can be said to exist if, within a system, 'no variable changes its position or relation with respect to the other variables'. This is a condition where the variables have adjusted to each other, having reached a 'steady or homeostatic state, enjoying a condition of harmony, stability or balance'. In systems where human beings are the actors, however, activity does not cease even when conditions of equilibrium have been achieved, and Easton considers 'the human participants to be in equilibrium when no individual or group changes its position *vis-à-vis* the other participants'.

Almond has admitted that the structural-functional cum equilibrium approach to social systems, in which it is assumed that 'families, economies, churches, polities tend to preserve their character through time, or to change slowly', can be subjected to a certain amount of criticism with which he would agree. He has consequently argued that though he would accept some of the criticisms as relevant, they should not be allowed to minimize the importance of the insights of structural-functionalists. His aim is to refine and elaborate on their original formulations.[14]

Almond claims furthermore that his work also has certain

specifically 'political science' antecedents, for he also wishes to revise the perhaps unsystematic but nevertheless functionalist analysis implicit in the writings of the authors of *The Federalist Papers* and in the work of the exponents of the interest group theories of politics.

CHARACTERISTICS OF POLITICAL SYSTEMS

All specifically *political* systems have, for Almond, four main structures which may be defined as 'legitimate patterns of interaction'.[15] Some structures may be more specialized than others, that is, perform fewer functions in the system. Secondly, whatever the differences between system and structures, the same political functions are performed in all political systems. Thirdly, the political structures perform a number of functions —they are 'multi-functional'. And finally, in the sense that all political systems, as parts of societies, are characterized by a culture, the culture is always a mixture of the modern and the traditional. Although as a system develops and its structures become more specialized there may be a diminution of the traditional aspects of its culture, these are never completely lost. Almond is therefore hesitant to analyse cultures and thus distinguished between societies in dichotomous terms, as Parsons and Levy have tended to do.

All political systems, then, regardless of their type, must perform a specific set of tasks if they are to remain in existence as systems in working order or in equilibrium (often then referred to as 'ongoing systems'). These are the functional requirements of the system. In various political systems, these functions may be performed by different kinds of political structures and, sometimes, even by structures which are not overtly recognized as being, primarily, 'political'. If one wishes to compare political systems, then, it is necessary to compare not simply their political structures, for these structures (a) may not actually be the mechanisms through which all the necessary functions are being performed or (b) they may not be performing the functions which had been earlier allotted to them—substitute structures may have developed to do this. This latter point is the one that Robert Merton, for example, emphasized in showing that in the United States, the 'political machine' developed over a period of time to perform certain functions (deemed necessary for the survival of the political system) which had, constitutionally, been allotted to other political institutions. A structure may cease to perform a particular function or set of functions, but it will be replaced by other structures; if this does not happen, the system will begin to disintegrate.

Since 'working' structures may be so elusive, especially where structures—patterns of interaction—may not be formally institutionalized, analysis is best begun by searching for phenomena which are known to be necessarily present in all systems: functions. It is best to begin analysis by asking a question of the following order: 'If such and such functions must be performed, through which mechanisms are these (mandatory) functions in fact being performed?' One searches for structures by asking questions about functions. This can be put in another way: one searches for institutions (formal or informal) by asking questions about *processes*.

This is the basis of Almond's structural-functional approach. It attempts to shift the locus of analysis from the observable institutional political mechanisms to any areas where the actual performance of the functional requirements of the systems are located. This approach is inclined to emphasize the search for processes that maintain the stability of the system. But Almond has claimed, in reply to criticism of this kind, that it can also lead the analyst to an awareness of the cases in which, for various reasons, the processes are not contributing to the 'well-being' of the system, but are inclining it to disequilibrium: that is, where processes become, in Merton's phrase, 'dysfunctional' to the system. Dysfunctional processes lead to strains which can either *change* the system or cause its disintegration.

Political systems can be compared in terms of the manner in which (the mechanisms or structures through which) functions are performed. In search of these functions, Almond found it useful to examine what he considers to be 'developed' (or 'modern') political systems—Western political systems. He concludes that all systems perform two basic sets of functions: *input* and *output* functions.[16] For Almond, the political system is made up of a set of roles, structures and subsystems, whose interactions are affected to a great extent by the psychological attributes and propensities of the actors involved. Moreover, the process can be seen in relation to its environment, so that the whole range of interactions can be interpreted as consisting of either *inputs* from the environment or from within the political process itself, or the *conversion* of these inputs within the system into *outputs* to the environment. Through time the outputs may produce environmental changes which may lead to new demands being made on the system or changes in the system itself. It is this notion of *feedback* which enables the systems theorist to incorporate in the analysis an account of the dynamic factors within political life which lead to change and development.[17]

Almond discerns four input functions and three output functions:

Input Functions:
1. Political socialization and recruitment
2. Interest articulation
3. Interest aggregation
4. Political communication

Output Functions:
5. Rule-making
6. Rule application
7. Rule adjudication

With respect to these, note first, that based as they are on modern Western (that is, liberal-democratic) systems, input functions are seen as being performed by non-governmental subsystems of the political system, the society and the general environment: by pressure groups, schools, political parties, independent newspapers and so on. On the other hand, the output functions are all governmental ones: it is governments and their bureaucracies which make rules (legislate), apply rules (administer) and adjudicate between individuals and groups on the basis of rules (laws, statutes etc). Thus the output functions, as Almond himself observes, bear a strong resemblance to governmental activity as defined in traditional separation-of-powers theory. Here is a case in which new concepts are devised for traditionally-recognized and otherwise named activities. The purpose of this is to shift the emphasis from description in terms of *institutions* which may be differently named in various countries and to substitute *one set* of functional concepts for describing the activities which these institutions perform, and which particular institutions may only perform momentarily.

Secondly, by introducing the concept of input, further emphasis is laid on the fact that the domestic political system of the state is not a 'closed' system whose working is determined solely by what happens within it; but more importantly, that the political system's activity is affected by other subsystems of the society *and* by processes and activities that occur in the wider environment beyond the borders of the state—by international relations. It will be recognized that 'input-output analysis' has, though obviously in a different way, been used by economists to analyse the working of domestic economic systems. (Economists have in fact preceded political scientists in this.[18])

Finally, we might note that at least two of the input functions, political socialization and political communication, are concerned with what we might call the creation and reinforcement of the realm of political values: the system of beliefs and ideas about the political system held by the individuals who participate in it. This 'psychological dimension of the political system', as Almond has called it, is referred to as the political culture.[19] This emphasis on the importance of values is an important component of structural-functional analysis, and stems, in part, from the work of Durkheim and Parsons.[20]

Models of Political Systems

Political systems can be compared in terms of the degree to which their political structures are specialized, that is, the degrees to which on the one hand specific functions are performed through particular structures or, on the other, to which a particular structure may perform a number of functions. In developed systems, then, structures are specialized, political roles are differentiated and functions are specific. This is the optimum condition, for since, as Almond points out, even modern systems are dual in their cultural characteristics (i.e. characterized by both traditional and modern aspects of their culture), here too will structures be found which are multifunctional, and boundaries between subsystems which are not well defined. Almond, in fact, remarks that in modern political systems 'the specialized structures of interest articulation (interest groups) aggregation (political parties) and communication (the mass media) exist in relation to persisting nonspecialized structures which are certainly modified by the existence of the specialized ones, but are by no means assimilated to them'. [21]

All political systems exist in societies which are in some degree culturally 'mixed' and so are themselves never totally, but more or less modern or more or less traditional. A developmental model assists us in distinguishing the extent of the 'mix' and gives us an indication of the points at which, for example, a traditional system begins to be characterized less and less by multi-functional structures and by diffuse boundaries between subsystems, and thus can be described as a 'transitional' system. But, at least as a general principle, it can be said that modern political systems are 'those in which there is a specialized political culture'. [22]

It is worth emphasizing, as we have already done, that the notion of *boundary* as here used (as with that of system) is not necessarily a geographical one. The boundary between the political system and its environment is not the same as that between the state and what happens beyond its *borders*. Boundaries may be determined between the political system and other subsystems (for example, social, economic, cultural) of the society and between various subsystems of the political system itself. These subsystems are all interdependent, though they can be seen, especially in modern political systems, as in some degree autonomous. The developmental states of the subsystems have a certain influence on the character of the political system. To take one example: for Almond, political systems attain to the characterization of 'modern' in part precisely because the societies of which they are a part and for which they cater have undergone certain irreversible transformations in their socio-economic structures. Such transformations are specific to each of these societies.[23]

PROCESSES OF ADAPTATION AND CHANGE

In his work following *The Politics of the Developing Areas*, Almond recognized a need for the refinement of the concept of political function and has attempted this by linking it with the ideas (developed by Easton) as to how political systems cope with the constant challenges of their environments. Systems operate at different levels of functioning: and '*the theory of the political system*' consists of a framework which identifies and explains 'the relations among these different levels of functioning—capabilities, conversion functions, and systems-maintenance and adaptation functions—and of the operation of the functions at each level' while '*the theory of political change*' deals with 'those transactions between the political system and its environment that affect changes in general system performance . . .'.[24]

The manner and mechanisms through which a political system converts inputs (for example, demands from various groups within it) and responds to, for example, processes in its environment, Almond calls the *conversion process*. The system's *capabilities* are denoted by the extent to which it can cope with inputs successfully. These conversion functions can be differentiated from those which are directed merely to the maintenance of the system itself: of these latter are, for example, the socialization and recruitment functions. The analysis of a system in terms of capabilities is one way of finding out the extent to which *in fact* a political system does possess the elements and mechanisms necessary for its survival. Thus Almond asserts, capabilities analysis is the method by which the empirical investigation of political systems is undertaken. It links the deductive analysis with the reality.[25] The system can be analysed by asking whether it possesses, and what is the state of, the *capacity* for extraction of resources, regulation of its elements (control over individuals and groups), distribution of resources (goods and services of various kinds) the capacity for the development and maintenance of symbols which increase attraction or loyalty to the system, and finally the capacity for responding adequately and in time to demands made upon it (for example for increased participation in the system).

But what brings about political change? From what sources are demands made upon the political system so that its capabilities are challenged? Almond identifies three sources: (1) from the elites within the political system itself; (2) from social groups in the environment; (3) from other political systems.[26] If we ask questions about the performance of functions, then we are led to seek the structures through which the functions are performed; then to ask how capably the structures are performing these functions (both maintenance and conversion ones). At this point we have the elements of an approach to the analysis of how political systems not only adapt but disintegrate or change in response to changes in their own and other environmental subsystems in terms of the efficiency of their capability and maintenance functions.[27] One could then be in a position to suggest (predict?) that some are likely to remain or to develop into stable systems, while others are likely to disintegrate momentarily and go through the process of changing from one type of political system to another, as distinct from the process of adaptation of a political system through gradual changes in its structure and capabilities.

For Almond, a political system is *stable* when the flow of inputs and outputs is such that inputs are converted in a way that does not result in any 'strains' being imposed on the system's capacity to respond to them, for such strains may have led the structure of the system itself to suffer basic changes; the outputs of the system then correspond adequately to the original demands. Those who have made demands then react to the outputs (for example, decisions made by government) 'in expected and legitimate ways'. Given the situation just described, 'the political system may be said to be *in a state of equilibrium* both internally (in the performance of conversion functions by political structures) and in its relations with its environments'.[28] Here, we might note, it would seem that, for Almond, the notion of equilibrium becomes not simply an explanatory concept, but a description of a realizable political situation.

CHAPTER V

David Easton's Analysis

In a book published in 1965 on *Politics in the Congo*, a student of African politics concluded that as far as the development, up to then, of systematic political theory was concerned, he could find no theory or set of theories sufficiently relevant to the explanation of political behaviour in the Congo of the post-independence period.[1] A year later, another student, in reviewing this work, suggested that political behaviour in the Congo seemed in fact susceptible to analysis in terms of the categories suggested by David Easton in his *A Systems Analysis of Political Life*, itself published in 1965.[2] Since then, a few other political scientists have also begun to suggest that Easton's work may be seen as providing an original set of concepts for arranging at the level of theory, and interpreting political phenomena in a new and helpful way.

To put these assessments in the context of the development of 'scientific method' we might note that the philosopher of science Stephen Toulmin has remarked that 'the heart of all major discoveries in the physical sciences is the discovery of novel methods of representation and so of fresh techniques by which inferences can be drawn—and drawn in ways which fit the phenomena under investigation'.[3] This, we find, is exactly what Easton has set out to do with respect to the analysis of the behaviour of political phenomena. He sees it as his task to 'identify a set of behaviours that . . . [can be described] as political, and, in the process, to construct an analytic system—a theory that would help to explain the behavioural reality'; for a political theory 'is but a *symbolic* system useful for understanding concrete or empirical political systems'.[4] And political theory of this kind can be referred to as 'empirical theory'.

The empirical theory which he wishes to devise he calls a *general* theory of politics: 'general' in two senses. First, Easton like other modern theorists rejects the idea that different kinds of theories need to be constructed to deal with national politics on the one hand and, for example, international politics, on the other. He sees no need for the traditional division of labour among students of politics. Instead it is necessary to develop what he calls a 'unified theory of politics' that is capable of explaining the behaviour of national and international political systems, and can also be used for comparing political systems.[5] Then the same propositions and categories could be applied to all kinds of political activities irrespective of the fact that there might be substantive differences between them. Secondly, Easton adheres to the view that the first task of political science is the analysis of the *general problems* common to all political systems, that is to say, primarily the analysis of the problem of the conditions under which political systems as systems survive over long periods of time, or to use his own phraseology, persist. The problem which students like Apter, and to some extent Almond and Coleman are concerned with, to wit—what are the prospects for the survival of *particular* kinds of governments or political orders, and how is the transition effected between one kind of order and another—Easton sees again as a substantive problem. If we deal with problems at this level we are in the realm of 'partial' rather than 'general' theory.

Easton, however, does not deny the importance of these substantive problems, but would hold that the solution of a number of substantive theoretical problems would not amount to the same thing as the solution of the problems with which general theory is concerned. Consequently the collecting of a number of partial theories does not in itself add up to the development of a general theory. For Easton, the main objective of general theory is 'to establish criteria for identifying the important variables requiring investigation in *all* political systems'.[6]

Next, Easton rejects the view that the most important type of political analysis is that which concerns itself with the power relations between the elements of a political system and the degree to which the 'benefits' provided by the political and governmental process are determined by the amount of 'power' or influence which an actor is able to command.[7] Thus, although Easton would agree that 'allocation' problems are of prime importance on a political system, and, indeed, while holding that what makes any act in society specifically political is that act's 'relation to the authoritative allocation of values for a society',[8] he would argue that 'allocation' analysis takes for granted that a political system has the capacity to exist over some period of time. The basis for Easton's argument is the fact that in 'allocation' analysis there is no problem about recognizing the political system as such for it is seen as unique and analytically quite different from any other type of system: its existence as a system is never held in doubt. Almond, for example, presents his readers with a list of system attributes and the main focus of his work is 'the authoritative allocation of values' within an ongoing, that is, persisting, system. For Easton it is this presumption of persistence that must first of all be questioned. He is far more concerned with the *conditions* of survival of political systems. Political science as a form of theory must concern itself, first, with the *existence* problems of political systems and then, not with a society's allocation of values, but with the allocation that is '*authoritative*'—that is, recognized as in some way legitimate.

Easton is also critical of the structural-functional approach on the grounds that the concepts which it provides are neither sufficient nor all-embracing enough to deal with all kinds of systems; further, its main concept, that of function, cannot be used as the basis of a theory, but simply as the prerequisite of any theory of systems, since the performance of some function is the minimum requirement of the behaviour of systems. The concept of function does, in fact, lack precision and is therefore difficult to apply empirically. In the field of anthropology, where the concept originated, the notion of function could be meaningfully used, because the systems being studied were relatively simple, homeostatic and isolated.[9] To be of use in studying modern, complex societies, these conditions either have to be assumed to exist (which they do not) or the concept of function has to be broadened and generalized and made so abstract that it becomes difficult, if not impossible, to use as a means of establishing causal relationships. Further, Easton's criticism in 1953 of 'equilibrium' analysis is relevant here. He argued that 'instead of viewing the state of equilibrium as a theoretical model, helpful in simplifying reality for purposes of analysis, rather than as an exact picture of reality', political scientists 'have committed the mistake of considering the equilibrium a possible condition of the empirical system'. Thus a 'heuristic device' was converted into a 'substantive description'. A 'heuristic device' might be some analytical framework, a theory or model, or simply a set of concepts used to assist in describing or explaining the existence or behaviour of some phenomenon. It does not, however, constitute a description of the phenomenon itself.[10]

Finally, we might note that Easton is concerned to uphold the view that there can be a *theoretical* study of politics—one dealing with the conditions of survival of political systems—as somewhat distinct from a political analysis that deals for example with the distribution of power and the allocation of values on the basis of this distribution. He would be critical of the Lasswellians for neglecting the theoretical as against the 'applied science' aspects of politics. It is, in his view, important that 'the *application* of knowledge' should not 'overshadow the discovery of general causal relations; at the most, it ought to play only a secondary role in the first stages of a social science'.[11]

In conjunction with his criticism of, for example, Lasswell, for taking *all* the allocation problems of a society as the relevant subject matter of political science, Easton dissociates himself from the view associated with Parsons that political theory can be analysed in terms of a 'general theory of social institutions'.

To allow this, would be to deny that political phenomena are characterized by certain specific kinds of relations, and may therefore be susceptible to analysis as a separate and distinct field. Rather, political life (and thus, the political system) is sufficiently autonomous—it is instituted by particular kinds of relations between phenomena which can be abstracted from general social relations—as to be an independent field of inquiry. 'Political science is the study of the authoritative allocation of values as it is influenced by the distribution and use of power.'[12]

PROBLEMS OF POLITICAL SCIENCE

Easton, then, can be said to view the discipline as he defines it as faced with two main problems: what we can call the *concrete* and the *theoretical*. And for these he recommends the systems analysis approach.

The concrete problem facing the political analyst is, as we have hinted, that concerning the 'persistence' of politics: how political systems manage 'to persist through time' in the face of the inevitable stress which they face. In political analysis, the central question to be answered is not how a particular political system persists in a given set of circumstances, but how political systems generally persist both in a stable environment and a changing world.[13]

If the concrete problem can be stated in this way *and* it is assumed that political life can in fact be seen as a system, then the theoretical problem that follows involves devising a *theoretical system*—a system of symbolic representations—for interpreting the 'life processes' of the system.[14] As Easton puts it, 'If we are to understand the way in which the behaving political system functions, what is the nature of the commitments we must make at the conceptual level, once we attribute systemic qualities to the actions that we . . . identify as constituting political life?'[15] It is the theoretical system that Easton variously refers to as the 'conceptual framework' or the 'structure of analysis', and this is distinct from the set of interacting elements—the concrete or empirical system which he refers to as the 'political system'. It is the process of interaction with which he is concerned; and he admits not to be greatly interested in the structure of behaviour or the structure of institutions as these words are used in, for example, Almond's analysis.

The systems analysis which Easton has developed is, he claims, based not on those characteristic of the 'old' social sciences such as sociology and economics: for example, his construction of an input-output framework bears, it is claimed, only superficial resemblance to that of economic analysis. Instead, he has drawn on the new 'communications sciences' and here, we might note, he has drawn for his inspiration on the same, or at least similar, sources as has Karl Deutsch.

THE METHOD OF ANALYSIS

What these new intellectual sources allow him to do, he thinks, is to formulate an approach—systems analysis—which is closer to that characteristic of the natural sciences than has formerly been the case in political science. For him, political activity is constituted of 'life processes' which can be analysed with as much success as the processes of living things. If his approach were successful, he would then have made a further step in linking the methods of the natural and social sciences. In fact, he is convinced that 'the perspectives of a systems analysis serve to link all of the sciences, natural and social'.[16]

In order to make statements of this nature, Easton would clearly have to show that there are properties which can be seen as common to both natural and social systems. He believes that political systems share a common characteristic, not only with other social systems, but also with some mechanical and biological systems. This is their ability to cope with most types of disturbance to which they may be subjected.[17] The political system, then, like living systems, is seen as a 'responding' and 'self-regulating' system. That is to say, it has within it mechanisms which allow it to change, correct and readjust its processes and structures in the face of activity which threatens to disrupt its own activity. Note that Easton makes a qualification: the elements of a political system need not, as in living systems and some mechanical ones, react automatically to disruptive or potentially disruptive activity. He only goes so far as to suggest that the elements or members of the political system possess the capability, though they do not always use it, to react to the stresses of their environment, so that they succeed in ensuring that 'some kind of system for making and executing binding decisions' persists.[18]

But the idea that political systems are self-regulating, regardless of the qualifications that he attaches to this claim, is one of the basic assumptions which allows Easton to claim that political life can be analysed as a system. A political system that is self-regulating can 'respond'—can adapt itself to environmental changes. It cannot only maintain its original equilibrium state, but can allow for changes in this state while retaining the characteristics that make it identifiable as the same political system. It is through this property that Easton attempts to distinguish his work from that of other systems analysts—perhaps, for example, the *early* Almond. For Easton, a system can change its structure and process if need be, in response firstly to stresses from its internal and external environment, and secondly to information that is the consequence of decisions (outputs) originally made by actors within the system. In other words, the system contains *feedback* mechanisms, that is, mechanisms capable of transmitting information of a positive or negative character to the system. They provide information about the reaction to decisions which have emerged within the system, and are thus instrumental in enabling the system to cope with these reactions in such a way as to ensure the persistence of the system. For Almond, however, changes within the system will eventually lead back to the *original* equilibrium state, whereas for Easton, a particular state of equilibrium can change whilst the political system still retains its identity as the same political system.

So Easton's systems analysis is that analytical framework (or, for him, theory) which explains why a system is capable of persisting; not simply of maintaining itself, but, if necessary, of adapting its structure to environmental stress.[19] Persistence, according to his definition, includes the idea that systems may change, and allows him to claim that his definition of a self-regulating political system implies a dynamic rather than the static analysis which he holds to be characteristic of the equilibrium approach. Hence also the importance of his continued emphasis on the fact that he is concerned with the basic 'life process' of the system and not with its structure. Structures may change, but life processes may remain, and in so far as they do, then the system continues to persist. It is in terms of these assumptions that Easton can claim that 'a system may persist even though *everything else associated with it* changes continuously and radically'.[20] He would no doubt hold, for example, that since, at least, the revolutions of the seventeenth century, the life processes of the British political system have persisted irrespective of changes in the structure of the system; thus the British political system has continued to persist.

Further, all this is comprehensible only in terms of the state that he sees as the antithesis of persistence, which is complete disintegration of the rule-making mechanisms. As he puts it, 'It helps us to understand what is meant by persistence if we interpret its negative to mean . . . that a system has disappeared completely. For the given society authoritative allocations of values could no longer be made.'[21] For example, such would be the case if all members of society were destroyed by some natural catastrophe or through annihilation by the use of modern means of warfare.

Certain other necessary terms of the analysis follow, with some of which we are already familiar. A political system is an *open* system, one that is receptive to the influences of its environment. At the analytical level it can be seen as separated from other societal systems by *system boundaries* which need not be geographical or otherwise empirically observable, but which can be distinguished in attempting to discern the relations between various patterns of activity. The *environment* of the political system is both intra-societal and extra-societal. It may be, since the political component of system is defined in relation to the authoritative allocation of values for a society, that what was once seen as part of the environment, may at some other time be seen as constituting part of the political system. Thus, for instance, an interest group such as the British Medical Association may be regarded for most of the time as part of the environment within which the political system operates; but when issues such as the remuneration of doctors or the extension of medical services provided by the state arise, the B.M.A. can be seen as part of the political system itself, trying to influence the 'authoritative allocation of values'. The system, an analytic concept, is to be defined in terms of the particular political problem or set of problems with which one is concerned.

The political system can be said to be in a *steady state* when it has arrived at an arrangement of its process which depends on some 'proper' balance between *inputs* and *outputs*.

It is interesting, in passing to note how similar this kind of proposed conceptual framework for political analysis is to that of the analysis of living things. Bertallanfy, for example has written that:

> From the standpoint of *Physics* the characteristic state in which we find the living organism can be defined by stating that it is not a closed system with respect to its surroundings, but an *open system* which continuously gives up matter to the outer world and takes in matter from it, but which maintains itself in this continuous exchange in a *steady state*, or approaches such a steady state in its variations in time . . .
>
> The organism as a whole is . . . never in true equilibrium, and the relatively slow processes of metabolism lead only to a steady state, maintained at a constant distance from time equilibrium by a continuous inflow and outflow, building up and breaking down of the component materials.[22]

Inputs can be defined briefly as constituted by the *demands* made upon the political system and the *supports* of the system itself.

Supports are those processes or structures which give it the capacity to cope with the demands made upon it. *Outputs* are the results of the processing of demands. Obviously there can be demands made upon the system as a result of the feedback process resulting from earlier outputs. There are influences acting on the political system (demands made upon it) which come from within the political system itself, for example from its political elite. Easton calls these 'withinputs', in order to distinguish them from those demand inputs that come from other systems of the society. In fact, the political system can, Easton claims, be seen basically as an input-output mechanism dealing with political decisions and the activities associated with these decisions: 'after all, in its elemental form a political system is just a means whereby certain kinds of inputs are converted into outputs'.[23]

Before going on to a description of the model, we must revert briefly to Easton's notion of 'the political'. His description of political science is determined by his definition of 'political life'—'a set or system of interactions defined by the fact that they are more or less directly related to the authoritative allocation of values for a society'; and a 'political system' then, is 'a set of interactions abstracted from the totality of social behaviour, through which values are allocated for a society'.[24] What makes a decision or policy 'political' is that the value allocations which are their consequences are 'authoritative'; and something (a decision, policy, or action) is deemed authoritative when those who are the subject of the decision, policy, or action, or who are affected by it, consider that it is imperative that they obey it.[25] This is a psychological rather than normative definition of, to use a traditional term, political obligation. Easton is not concerned with why people ought to obey, nor even why they feel they ought to obey (except to the extent that this influences their behaviour) in a political system, but merely with the fact that they do so, and with discovering the conditions underlying a political system that incline people to find it opportune to obey.

Note also that when he uses the term 'values' (allocation of values) he does not necessarily use it in the sense in which Parsons or Almond use the term *value system*—a system of ideas, beliefs. Rather, his use[26] is nearer that of economists: one allocates a value—a price or worth—to a thing, and the normative element of value, which need not necessarily be present at all, is not of major importance to the analyst. Every society is faced with the problem of authoritative policy formation, and it is the numerous arrangements for and outcomes to this problem in different societies that provide the subject-matter of the student of politics. This is what Easton refers to as the 'authoritative allocation of values'. Political science thus becomes, *inter alia,* a study of the distribution by persons in authority of things which are valued, or the attribution by such persons of value to things, or the deciding by such persons of disputes relating to things which are valued.

It will be observed that another key term in the definition of political system is that of 'interaction' which Easton calls 'the basic unit' of his analysis: interactions, and not Parsons' 'actor' or Almond's 'role', for Easton's emphasis is on processes rather than structures. He is interested not in unit actions, but in *exchanges* (of inputs) and *transactions* across system boundaries.

EASTON'S MODEL OF THE POLITICAL SYSTEM
One of the main characteristics of the political system as an open system is that it is constantly subjected to challenges from its environment, with which it is required to cope. In other words, its life processes may constantly be subjected, in Easton's phrase, to *stress* from the environment. The purpose of constructing a model of the political system is precisely to assist us in understanding how political systems are able to persist in the face of this stress—in understanding the mechanisms in terms of which the political system responds.

Easton asserts that there are two kinds of stress to which the political system may be subjected, and that the system is capable of various kinds of response, by means of which the stress can be coped with—response mechanisms at both the cultural and the structural level. The manner in which such stress may affect a system can be described as follows: stress on a system from within, or from its environment, may be such that those conversion processes which provide the system with a capacity for persistence may be affected; if as a result, those outputs of the system which relate to the making and executing of binding decisions are not forthcoming, then the system has ceased to function. It has 'broken down'.[27] The two main types of stress are (*a*) demand stress and (*b*) support stress.

Demand stress may result either from the failure of the system as it exists to cope successfully with the information feedback from its original output, or from the system's incapacity to deal with the particular range of demands made upon it: in other words, the system may be subjected to 'demand-input overload'. This overload may take place in terms of the volume of demands, the content or nature of the demands or it may be that the inflow of demands *at some particular time* is too great for the system to take in.[28]

All political systems are subject to *support stress* at some time; by which is meant that the system may suffer a loss, or at least an erosion, of the support given to it by the members of the system. This may result from cleavages among members within the system; failure of the system to produce outputs in response to demands made upon it or to produce outputs satisfactory to its members; or from some structural failure of the system itself, for example as a result of the failure of the institutional structure to cope with demands for universal participation within the system.[29] All systems, Easton holds, are characterized by a 'critical range' beyond which stresses upon them affect their functioning so as to cause their disintegration. At this point the 'essential variables' of political life—'the allocations of values for a society and the relative frequency of compliance with them' are affected in such a manner that political life itself becomes impossible.[30]

If the supports of a political system are deemed necessary to its existence then there must be some structural bases of these

supports (institutional—electoral arrangements, party structures, etc. or non-institutional—the norms and expectations
which affect individuals' or groups' behaviour, for example,
such as the set of attitudes or predispositions associated with
patriotism or party loyalty), and similarly the system must be
constituted of some structure to which support is given. It is in
this context, that Easton, though emphasizing that he is concerned mainly with processes, arrives at analysis of what might
be called the main structures of the political system, but which
he prefers to refer to as the *objects of support* of the system. Again,
however, the important point is, that he is not concerned with
the structures peculiar to particular types of political systems
(which is, for example, one of the main preoccupations of David
Apter's work), but with those necessary to the existence and persistence of all kinds of political systems (or to 'the political
system', used as a generic term).

The main structures or objects of support of the political
system are three: the *political community*, the *regime*, and the
authorities. These are distinct entities: 'Authorities typically
come and go, regimes or constitutional orders may change. In
both cases the community may remain quite stable . . . But political communities are capable of changing. This occurs at
moments when the membership undergoes some internal sub-
division indicating that whole groups have withdrawn their support from the pre-existing division of political labour.'[31]

Where a group of people come together and show some
degree of willingness to co-operate in solving the problems of the
political system, there we have a *political community*. As a means
to making the system work, the community is characterized by a
political division of labour. The political community is one of
the main, if not *the* main component of the system, for where
there is a decline in support for the political community, then it
is likely that the political system will be subjected to stress.
Easton distinguishes between the political community and what
he calls 'the sense of community' a term he uses to illustrate the
corpus of sentiments and beliefs which individuals have about

involvement in the political community. He does, however, wish to stress that the sense of community is not a *necessary* element of the political community. Individuals may be involved in that political division of labour which is the political community without necessarily sharing to any great degree similar values. The sense of community is not, in the short term, a necessary prerequisite for the persistence of a political community. Easton is concerned to distinguish his definition from the more socio-logically-informed definitions of community which stress the importance of shared values. [32]

The regime of the political system could be called the 'constitutional order' as that term is used with reference to the government of Britain: it is that set of ideas/rules (written and unwritten) and sentiments which indicates that there is some regularized and predictable method for dealing with political problems. Easton wishes to avoid the impression that the regime is simply a structure; it is in fact, for him, composed of values, norms and structures. [33]

What Easton refers to as the *authorities* are the group of individuals who over some period of time assume the responsibility for making governmental decisions. He distinguishes between the 'authorities' and the 'structure of authority' or roles which the authorities assume: he is concerned with the former, for his point of reference is what those in authority do rather than the structure or institutional framework within which they act. [34]

It is the authorities who, in the political system, have to process the inputs from the internal and external environment into outputs (decisions, actions), and who in turn, have to cope with the information (whether in the form of new supports or demands) that is the outcome of the original outputs. Nevertheless the political system may be constituted of various other subsystems, such as mediating groups which are involved in the conversion process: for example, in coping with stresses before these reach the level of the authorities. 'Many of the conflicting demands over scarce values will be settled as the result of autonomous interaction among individuals and groups themselves.'[35] These subsystems are made up of the activities of partial associations in society which Easton refers to as parapolitical systems, for example, those activities of trade unions, churches, automobile associations, etc. which relate to the allocation of scarce resources or the framing of policies to govern the use of resources. Obviously, however, the degree of support of the authorities is an important indication of the system's potential for persistence.

There have been, as yet, few attempts to operationalize Easton's model, his own empirical work being in the main concerned with political socialization, with the analysis of how the values which are an important component of the regime come to be acquired by individuals. An interesting attempt has, however, been made to analyse the incipient development and working of a European Political Community as a political system in terms of the concepts formulated and ordered by Easton.[36] This is a level of analysis which would seem particularly relevant to the model, for it deals with an area where there is as yet no geographically bounded and constitutionally defined political system. Here, the groups involved in the 'political division of labour' are not readily observable and the political system is itself still elusive.

CHAPTER VI

David Apter's Analysis

The emergence of new nations in the postwar era has provided a focus of interest for many students of politics. The end of colonialism and the appearance of new sovereign states has given new impetus to many of the traditional queries of the political scientist, such as inquiries about the characteristics of authority in political systems. These developments also produced new questions uniquely related to the emergent situation, concerning the processes involved in the transition from one type of political system to another.

These 'concrete' problems led to a related emphasis on the development of appropriate methods and concepts to enhance our understanding of the various aspects and levels of the process of transition. Analyses of the 'concrete' problems and the development of appropriate analytic methods and techniques have evolved simultaneously. The work of David Apter reveals this dual interest.

With his work, we are back not only to the study of political systems in 'systemic' terms, but also to the classification and analysis of types of government. In fact the elements of the social system are analysed mainly for the purpose of understanding the extent to which particular types of governments or systems of authority operate best only in particular kinds of social environment; and how changes in elements, or relations between the elements of the social system influence changes in governmental systems. His subject is the study of 'the politics of modernization' which, he tells us, 'requires the unity of moral and analytical modes of thought'.[1]

Clearly, a statement of this kind already implies a form of analysis different from that of Easton, who although he had earlier written that a theoretical framework for the study of politics would, among other things, suggest 'categories for examining the moral premises out of which the theory emerged',[2] seems not to have grappled with this problem in his later work. But more than this, an analysis that deals with types of government and the extent to which it is possible to choose between them is more likely to involve itself in a consideration of the moral problems of politics, than is a systemic analysis which has as one of its assumptions a psychological definition of political obligation. 'I believe', Apter writes, 'that politics begins with models that are primarily normative and secondly empirical.'[3]

The assumptions which lead Apter to this point of view are important. The central assumption is that the most important problem requiring analysis in the social sciences is that of how *choices* are made. And the peculiar problem for political science, is that politics, unlike the other forms of social relations, 'begins with the moral aspects of choice'. What Apter refers to as 'modernization' he perceives as beginning where any societal culture allows individuals to develop a critical view of man in his relation to nature and society; then men begin to see life as involving different kinds of choices—personal, social or structural and moral.[4]

The main difference between governmental choices and other kinds of choices made in a society is that the choices of government generally have implications and consequences for all the members of that society, and, moreover, bind all the members, for government is 'the most generalized membership unit' which has 'defined responsibility for the maintenance and/or adaptation of the system of which it is a part'.[5] Those choices made by government and which are accepted by the society over a period of time, can be said to constitute the 'moral aims' of the society.

Thus although, as we shall see, Apter wishes to use for

analysis the modern tools of social science, and in this sense aligns himself with modern political theorists, he emphasizes, by his statement of the problem which concerns him, that he is intent on analysing problems and seeking the answers to questions familiar to traditional theorists. For him certain types of government are indeed better suited than others to the solution of particular political problems and to the attainment of particular societal aims. Similarly, he would argue that certain types of government are indeed likely to be more stable in the long term than others. And the types of government which exist are to be seen not simply as the inevitable consequences of certain structural conditions of society, but must, in part, also be seen as being the result of deliberate choices by men, choices made in the context of ideas held about the end of man in a society. The following statement by Apter would, then, hardly sound strange to those familiar with the works of the 'masters of political thought': '. . . the political types employed here are to be viewed first as *moral tendencies* reflecting the perpetual tension between two fundamentally different conceptions of man in society, the secular-libertarian and the sacred-collectivity'.[6]

The immediate impetus inclining Apter to this kind of definition of his problem and to the form of analysis which he has devised to deal with it, came, we may surmise, from the problems found in his study of the development of governmental systems in the colonial and later autonomous regions of Africa. Here, as Almond has explained, was a mixed if not confused social and political context: a variety of cultural systems, mainly traditional with the beginnings of modernity; differing rates of social change brought on by the introduction of economic and educational development; 'modern' colonial systems of government superimposed on traditional forms of tribal government. Apter was concerned to observe, in his studies of the Gold Coast and Uganda, how modern systems were grafted on to traditional (or largely traditional) social systems and how in turn the traditional system of government adapted itself, if at all, to the modern. The primary problem, as he defined it, was how the process of 'political institutional transfer' was effected in colonial territories.[7]

There was a second problem—the theoretical one—to match the concrete problem just described. This we have referred to as the Bagehotian problem.[8] As Apter defined it in his study of Uganda: '. . . if we are not to follow after events with *post hoc* explanations which change with every variation in political arrangements, we need a set of abstractions which will help us find our way through the exciting multiplicity and complexity of change'.[9]

The development of political institutions in colonial countries, ex-colonial countries, and in states with forms of social structure broadly similar to the latter, is in the modern era directed to the resolution of two problems which, for Apter, all governments come up against: that of ensuring that change in general is as orderly as possible, taking place in a manner that is in some degree predictable; and that of ensuring that the holders of governmental authority succeed each other in a peaceful fashion. Generally, these problems have to be resolved at the same time as attempts are being made to resolve other problems brought to light as a result of social and economic changes. In the developing countries, this mixture of political, economic and other social problems is perhaps most obvious, and so they present, as it were, a laboratory for extensive scientific analysis, if not experiment. This context provides the social scientists with an opportunity to suggest a variety of theories which can in turn be tested, adapted, verified or rejected. These theories are perhaps, in Easton's terminology, partial rather than general; but Apter emphasizes the tentativeness of his work up to this point.

Apter makes a further distinction (which we do not see in Easton's work, for example) between scientific analysis in the social sciences and that in the natural sciences. This is not a distinction in terms of technique, but, as he puts it, 'in the moral point of view'. Social acts, and thus political acts, have meaning for the actors themselves, and the meanings which they attrib-

ute to their actions themselves have implications and consequences. The political analyst therefore requires not only
scientific knowledge, but a certain degree of 'moral intuition'
if he is to make a satisfactory analysis.

Apter's estimation of the problems which require analysis,
and his particular assumptions about the proper scientific
method for political investigation (assumptions which precede
and in fact condition the development of the conceptual framework), lead him to focus the analysis of the myriad of problems
in terms of a general problem: that which he calls
'modernization'. More specifically, he is concerned with the
effect of the process of modernization of the social structure on
the process of politics and on the development of forms of
government, and then with the extent to which those in authority are able to make choices (even about the types of government which they require) within the context of various forms of
ever-changing social structures.

Modernization, for Apter, is to be distinguished from both
development in general and industrialization. It is a 'particular
case' of the process of development. Development can be
defined as a process involving the increased specialization of
functional roles in a society. The society is also characterized by
increasing secularization. Industrialization, which Apter sees as
a part of the process of modernization, is related by him to the
development of roles specifically related to the manufacturing
process. Industrialization, in general, follows (is a consequence
of) modernization; for modernization presupposes a particular
social framework which, in turn, is a prerequisite to industrialization.[10]

Modernization, then, is a process that occurs predominantly
in non-industrial societies where 'it may be described as the
transposition of certain roles—professional, technical, administrative—and the transposition of institutions supporting those
roles—hospitals, schools, universities, bureaucracies'.[11] For the
process of modernization to begin, the social system must be inclined to accept and encourage innovation, the social structures

of the system must have begun, at least, to be differentiated, and the system must be one which encourages or is beginning to encourage the development of technological skills. The increasing complexity of the society as a result of all this leads to an increase in the complexity of the political problems of the society.[12]

Thus 'the politics of modernization'—the way in which the political system and, more particularly, government reacts to the problems of modernization—constitutes by itself a sufficient, interesting and important subject for study. 'Modernization,' Apter has written, resorting to metaphor to describe the process, 'is like hurtling through a tunnel at frightening speed without knowing what waits at the other end. Fear creates serious political problems.'[13] Here, as in Almond's work, there is a suggestion of teleological analysis, but one that does not specify a *particular* end. The process is 'open-ended'.

If, for Apter, modernization has to do with changes and development of roles we have already a small hint of the type of analysis to which he may be inclined. Like Almond he is in favour of a structural-functional analysis. However since roles are no more than 'institutionalized forms of *behaviour* defined by functions', then there needs to be added to structural-functionalism, some other form of analysis which deals with the motives underlying behaviour.[14] To this end, Apter is also inclined to a form of behavioural analysis.

All this can be put in a slightly different way. If at the level of the concrete there is perceived a dual problem for political analysis—(*a*) the analysis of choice and (*b*) the analysis of the context in which choices take place, then, Apter suggests, at the analytical level itself a dual approach is required. This approach is one that incorporates both the structural and the behavioural approaches.

THE METHOD OF ANALYSIS

Apter states it as the aim of his analysis to examine the conditions under which it is possible for governments to maintain

their authority during the period of modernization. He is therefore concerned with the problem of legitimacy: the relation, at
various times, between the authority of a government and the
degree of support that it is able to engender. What is noticeable
in this statement is that, unlike the authors whom we have considered—even other structural–functionalists—the emphasis is
as much on the *institution of government* as it is on the structural or
systemic basis of government.[15]

Governments can be described and distinguished in terms of
two main properties: (1) the degree of centralization of the
system of authority, or as Apter calls it, the degree of 'hierarchy', and (2) the kind of system of values to which those in
authority adhere, and which they may try to make generally
accepted throughout the political system and society. Now, the
choice of a government with a particular degree of hierarchy
and a particular system involves, Apter stresses, normative decisions, even though the structural foundations of a society may be
more conducive to one form of government than another. In
other words, choices about types of government are, in part at
least, moral choices, and this is why Apter wishes to devise a
theory that is *normative* as well as structural and behavioural.

Thus the types of government which Apter posits as his limit-
ing types (he describes them as 'ideal types' at the extreme ends
of a continuum) he refers to as 'normative' systems, each one of
which is characterized by particular structural features and
whose modes of political and civil life are of a specific kind.[16]
These models of government—the *sacred-collectivity* model and
the *secular-libertarian* model—are delineated in terms of the two
criteria already mentioned: hierarchy and value-system. Every
type of government, Apter suggests, can also be seen as involving a particular form of relationship between the level of *coercion*
which characterizes the political system and society and the
amount of *information* which is allowed to percolate through
them, and the amount of both information and coercion is
related to the extent of hierarchy and the kind of values characteristic of the governmental order. It is, in fact, the relationship

between information and coercion that determines the degree of *choice* which is open to government.[17]

Finally, the legitimacy of a government is the result of the degree to which it is deemed both moral (the extent to which it sets and achieves goals deemed normatively satisfactory) and efficient; and, conversely, only if it is deemed legitimate is it, in the long run, able to achieve the goals which it posits. Legitimacy, therefore, is in Apter's words, 'derived from two types of values, *consummatory* and *instrumental*'. Consummatory values are those which have their basis in moral preconceptions; and instrumental values those which relate to the performance of activities according to particular criteria of efficiency.

THE TYPES OF GOVERNMENT

As reviewers of Apter's work have remarked, the two pure types which he posits do bear some resemblance to the so-called totalitarian (or at least, highly authoritarian) and liberal-democratic types of government in relation to which present-day contemporary governments tend to be described. In any case, it is Apter's view that present-day modernizing societies do not possess the structural basis to support either totalitarian or liberal-democratic systems of government.

Instead in these modernizing societies governments and political systems are likely to develop forms different in kind from, but in some characteristics approaching, either of the two models. Apter suggests that these be referred to as 'accommodated political systems'; they vary greatly in composition, and should be viewed as 'pre-democratic' rather than 'anti-democratic'. An important assumption here is that liberal-democratic institutions may just not be suitable, or to put it another way, have failed to survive, in modernizing societies, an assumption which was perhaps reinforced for Apter by his studies of Ghana and Uganda. By referring to these countries as 'pre-democratic' there is, he suggests, an assumption or an implication that 'certain institutions of coercion' can be viewed as '*perhaps necessary* to the organization and integration of a modernizing community'.[18] This itself suggests a *stages analysis*, in which it is recognized that certain properties necessary to political practices at one stage of development, may simply not be present in a society during some previous period. To recognize this is important, for one of Apter's major concerns is that the political scientist should 'know the direction in which society is headed in order to understand the basis on which its authority rests'.[19]

Basically, there are two broad models of 'accommodated political systems': the *reconciliation system* which approximates to the secular-libertarian end of the continuum and the *mobilization system* which approximates the sacred-collectivity model. These types involve certain commitments to ways in which a political community ought to operate. For example the government of a reconciliation system attempts to attain goals which 'fit' the prevailing value system of the society; while that of a mobilization system, which tends to revolutionize the existing society, attempts to impose a new and cohesive system of values on the society.

There are still other variants of these broad types: what Apter refers to as the 'modernizing autocracy', the 'military oligarchy' and the 'neo-mercantilist society'. It is his view that the types most likely to be characteristic, in the long run, of modernizing societies are the 'modernizing autocracy' and the 'neo-mercantilist society'. These are 'optimal political forms for long-term modernization, in particular, for the conversion from the "early" to the "late" stages of the process'.[20] The reconciliation system, on the other hand, he uses as the generic term that covers the political system in modern industrial societies.

A large part of Apter's work is devoted, then, not only to classification, but to demonstrating how types of governmental system in modernizing societies develop, and how it is possible for one type to change into another, for 'if government is the critically strategic unit of a system, then failures of government will imply failures of the entire system'.[21] Further, he is concerned with the development of and changes which occur in various kinds of political parties, for the party he sees as a 'critical force for modernization in all contemporary societies'.

If political parties are important, and are even major mechanisms for effecting change in modernizing societies, then the ideologies and 'political religions' which those in authority adhere to must be analysed,[22] as must the political predilections of those who exercise authority. A description of a governmental system must, then, make reference to all these variables. Thus, for example, Apter views the neo-mercantilist system as a form of corporate state, similar to, or having a tendency to become, a presidential monarchy, in which there exists a one-party government and a system of charisma that has been ritualized.[23] But government exists in the wider context of the political system and of society; and in so far as it is seen as a critical factor in the ordering, preservation and shaping of society, there are certain functions which must be performed if any type of government is to continue to survive. (According to Apter, government is 'a concrete structural requisite for any social system . . . [it] is the most strategic substructure'.[24]) Apter's analysis, therefore, like any other structural-functional one, involves the search for the functional and structural requisites of government. The two functional requisites are seen as the provision of *information* and the presence of a 'practical monopoly of *coercion*'. In any system an inverse relation exists between these.

Further, Apter suggests, all governmental systems are characterized by a number of *contingent functions*. These indicate the extent of identity and solidarity in the society, and so are also indicators of the viability of the governmental system itself. All governments must act as (1) the loci of sanctions in a society, (2) the providers of symbols linking a people's past and future, (3) the responsible agents for the 'orderly arrangement and performance of roles in the system', (4) the providers of criteria for deciding on membership and participation in the society.[25]

There are, finally, two main structural requisites of government. All governments are characterized by a 'structure of authoritative decision-making' and a 'structure of accountability'. These are simply, in other words, the main institutional requirements of government. Similarly, all governmental systems possess contingent structures which give an indication of the efficiency of the system. These are really 'substructures' of the structural requisites and include mechanisms for political recruitment, rule enforcement and role delimitation, the allocation and determination of resources and some mechanism through which, at some official level, government registers societal approval of its decisions and policies (a parliament or a central committee for example). In effect, contingent structures are mechanisms for carrying out *policy*.

The structural patterns or context of the modernizing society are discussed by Apter under three main headings: the state of the 'traditional' system, the effect of modernization on its stratification patterns and the trends to be discerned in the development of careers—or, in other words, in the development of the notion of 'professionalism'. We will mention an aspect of this here, that is, his insistence on the importance of the *intellectual* in modernizing societies, and his view that as the process of modernization continues, the pragmatist—in fact the technician or expert—replaces both the generalist and the more purely 'political intellectual' or ideologue. 'Our contention has been', he writes, 'that fundamental modernization processes, despite the appearance of confusion and mixing, tend towards a peculiar kind of confrontation, which is reflected and located in the organization of career roles in the various modernizing systems. *At its widest limits, the modernization process is the confrontation of the ideologue and the scientist . . .*'[26] Apter accepts the view that the new 'careerists' are inclined to an ideology of rationalism and scientific method, and, at the level of the solution of societal problems to, in Karl Popper's phrase, the ideology of 'social engineering'. This elite is to be distinguished from the group Apter refers to as the 'intellectuals', the group 'most inclined to respect the culture of freedom'. The position of intellectuals in relation to other groups in a modernizing society can, for Apter, be taken as an indication of the form that the political system will take.[27]

CONCLUSION

At first sight, Apter's analysis seems less 'systemic' than those of the other writers whom we have considered. But this impression may have been gained simply because his scheme is by far the most detailed, and, moreover, specific to the analysis of a particular problem of political behaviour: the choice and development of governments in modernizing societies. Further, he has laid great emphasis on what, for him, is the necessary normative element of political theorizing. He also makes a 'speculation' on the prospects for the development of what he calls 'political democracy' in modernizing societies—a speculation that is again uncharacteristic of the theorists whose work we have earlier described. For Apter, a distinction can, and must, be made between the method of theorizing in the social sciences and in the natural sciences; and he seems less inclined to suggest that the 'scientific method' to which he undoubtedly adheres is, necessarily and only, the same as the methodology of the natural sciences.

CHAPTER VII

Karl W. Deutsch's Analysis

If it should prove possible, as David Easton has suggested, to devise a theory of the behaviour of political phenomena that can provide a complete explanation of the basic processes of those phenomena—whether they be found within the state or beyond its borders—then the work of Karl Deutsch will have constituted one of the major steps in this direction. For perhaps his primary assumption, as with Easton, is that developments in the new communications sciences have led to a diminution in importance of the differences, for analytical purposes, between the behaviour of living things and that of social organizations. There has, consequently, he would also argue, been at least a lessening in the gulf between the methods used by natural scientists on the one hand, and social scientists on the other. Concepts and methods drawn from the new sciences can now, without fear of being misleading, be used to analyse the behaviour of organizations, and Deutsch sees the state, as well as other types of political systems as, fundamentally, types of organizations.

His aim, then, is to use the concepts and methods of the science of cybernetics to provide explanations for, not simply the survival but the *growth* of political systems, and to predict the consequences of changes that affect the structures of systems. His work can, in a sense, be seen as an explanation of some of the assumptions underlying that of Easton, as well as an attempt to refine and further develop (if perhaps in a slightly different direction) the analysis of 'life processes' of the political system that Easton has undertaken.[1]

Underlying Deutsch's view of the kind of methodology that is relevant to political analysis is a particular view of political activity, the state as a political system and the government of political systems.

It is one of the concerns of Deutsch to reduce the importance of the notion of *power* as a component of continuing political activity and thus as a (or *the*) decisive element in definitions of 'politics'. This is not because he denies that power—the capacity of an individual, for example, to compel another to do what he wills—is an important aspect of political activity; but because he wishes to reduce, it seems, the significance of the 'physical force' aspect in definitions of power. Power Deutsch sees as 'neither the centre nor the essence of politics'. Rather, as Parsons has also suggested, 'It is one of the currencies of politics, one of the important mechanisms of acceleration or of damage control *where influence, habit, or voluntary co-ordination may have failed*, or where these may have failed to serve adequately the function of goal-attainment.'[2] This characterization of power gives us a clue to how Deutsch views politics and political systems.

Politics is concerned with the attainment of social goals; it is the sphere in which decisions are made with respect to the whole society—decisions which are enforceable. The 'core-area' of politics is 'the area of enforceable decisions'; and the 'essence of politics' for Deutsch is the 'dependable co-ordination of human efforts for the attainment of the goals of society'. It is a process through which a society decides that certain activities are preferable to others and should be carried out. But the enforcement of decisions about the direction of society depends not simply on the threat of force exercised by those who possess it, but perhaps more importantly in the long run, on the fact that for members of the society it has become habitual to comply with the decisions of those in authority.[3]

That the carrying out of governmental decisions can be shown over a period of time to be due to 'habit' as much as to threat, is for Deutsch an indication of the fact that society and the political system survive and develop at least partly because they contain mechanisms which allow or encourage habit-forming and the other activities that go with this: the acquiring of information; the selection and storage of this information (the facility of memory); the selection and development of norms relating to the use of information gained. It is through characterizing society in this manner that Deutsch is able to conclude that, for example, *'the inner source of political power*—the relatively coherent and stable structure of memories, habits and values depends on existing facilities for social communication, both from the past to the present and between contemporaries',[4] and to suggest that in a political system, 'information precedes compulsion'.[5]

If the amount and spread of information and the strength of the mechanisms for the communication of information are the important indicators of the existence of a community or a society, then with respect to politics, that is, with respect to the making and enforcement of decisions for the society as a whole, the *system* of decision making and enforcement (*the political system*) can be seen as a 'network of communication channels'.[6] It is like any other system, one in which on the basis of information gained and stored over a period, its components (in this case individuals, groups, nation-states) come to act and react in accordance with expectations about how others will act and react. The political system, for Deutsch, 'depends to a large extent on the fabric of co-ordinated expectations'.[7]

New political systems, as communications systems with processes and mechanisms for the acquisition, collection, transmission, selection, and storage of information, developed over a period of time, can be seen, Deutsch maintains, in some degree as 'self-regulating' or 'self-controlling' systems. The members of the political system come to acquire mechanisms for the transmission of messages and for the co-ordination and control of the channels of communication. The cohesion of a political system can then be analysed in terms of the degree to which these co-ordination and control mechanisms continue to function properly—to adapt themselves, in the context of the goals which they set, to the information which they receive from various sources; and even to modify the goals which they have set themselves.

Self-regulation and control involve the direction of information into or away from particular communication channels, rather than the shifting of 'wills' through threats of force: that is, they involve the 'steering' of information, rather than the exercise of power over individuals. Deutsch writes that, 'essentially, control involves the transmission of messages, and the understanding of control processes is a branch of communications engineering, not of power engineering'.[8] *Government* then, for Deutsch, ought to be seen as involving this kind of steering rather than as involving, predominantly, the use of power. Looked on in these terms, he maintains, government in a political system and of a society is analogous to the steering of a ship; it is a form of administration of communication channels. It might be more profitable at the level of analysis, he suggests, 'to look upon government somewhat less as a problem of power and somewhat more as a problem of steering; and ... steering is decisively a matter of communication'.[9]

Three points ought to be noticed here. First, Deutsch also views the subsystem (parties, interest groups), as, so to speak, miniature communications systems, interconnected and open, but also to some extent capable of steering themselves and with mechanisms (human and institutional) that allow them to adapt and modify their structures and behaviour. Similarly, conflicts between political systems or between subsystems can then be seen not simply as contests of 'wills' (in the sense that the term 'will' is traditionally used), but as the consequence of collisions caused, for example, because of failures of steering facilities or of the signals of the systems.

Secondly, the concept of growth of a political system must be understood also in these terms. It indicates the capacity of a system to apply the information that it has acquired (to apply its 'learning capacity') to (1) increasing its openness, that is to refining the channels through which it receives information; (2)

increasing its capacity to respond effectively to its environment; and (3) increasing 'the range and diversity' of the goals which it has the capacity to set itself to pursue and achieve.[10]

Finally, we can deduce that for Deutsch, a society or a political system that is to be seen as a 'self-steering' organization, must be viewed as a historical system, that is to say, it must possess memory. There is a hint of Edmund Burke here, though Deutsch decisively rejects the 'classical organic' view of politics associated with that writer. Nevertheless, a society must, if it is to be self-steering, receive information from three sources: 'from its past', from its external environment (it must be an open system) and from its internal environment (that is, information about the state and behaviour of its own parts). The flow of information must be continuous.[11]

SOURCES OF THE APPROACH

The science which deals with steering—with the control of information flows—is the comparatively new one of cybernetics, and the concepts which Deutsch uses to describe political phenomena are drawn from this. He is able to perceive similarities in processes and functional requirements between living things, electronic machines and social organizations, and having rejected the other models of political analysis, suggests that cybernetics analysis is relevant to the understanding of social systems, since they do in their processes 'resemble' other types of organizations. The brain, the computer, the society all have characteristics which make them organizations: they have the capacity to transmit and react to information. The model of the cybernetic system can therefore replace 'the classic analogues or models of mechanism, organization, and process, which so long have dominated so much of scientific thinking'.[12]

Cybernetic analysis (so-called by Norbert Weiner[13]) was developed and made possible by developments over the past thirty years or so in a number of disciplines: neurophysiology, psychology, mathematics, electrical engineering. It is, as one writer puts it, 'concerned with ways in which certain kinds of apparatus are maintained through "feedbacks", that is to say devices by which the entropy of a system is counteracted by returning some of its output into input'.[14] From this description one sees the similarities in the bases of the Easton and Deutsch approaches. Both writers see cybernetics or communications models as contributing to a linking of the science of living things, that of self-regulating machines, and that of social systems. All the systems involved can be viewed as networks of inter-connected parts, the patterns of the network being in fact patterns of information flows.[15]

A cybernetic model directs the analyst to specific aspects of any system. He is led, for example, to analyse the amount of variety of information; the structure of the information network (information, Deutsch remarks, represents a 'patterned relationship between events'); the structure of subsystems; the feedback system; the organization of the system's 'memory' mechanisms; and the rules which determine the behaviour of the system.

THE METHOD OF ANALYSIS

A key concept which Deutsch (like Easton) claims distinguishes his approach from the equilibrium approach is that of *feedback*. By feedback 'or as it is often called, a servo-mechanism—is meant a communications network that produces action in response to an input of information, *and includes the results of its own action in the information by which it modifies its subsequent behaviour*'.[16] All organizations are characterized by feedback mechanisms. The presence of these mechanisms allows the organization to change its state if necessary in reaction to information, rather than, as in equilibrium systems, simply to react in such a manner as to attempt to return to its original state. In equilibrium theories, as Deutsch understands them, growth or evolution of system states is not allowed for. The introduction of the concept of feedback, therefore, Deutsch argues, introduces the element of dynamism into what would otherwise be a static analysis.

As subconcepts of the feedback concept, Deutsch introduces those of negative feedback, load, lag, gain and lead. A *negative feedback* system is one which transmits back to itself information which is the result of decisions and actions taken by the system, and which leads the system to change its behaviour in pursuit of the goals which it has set itself. *Load* indicates the total amount of information which a system may possess at a particular time. *Lag* indicates the amount of delay which the system experiences between reporting the consequences of decisions and acting on the information received. *Gain* is an indication of the manner in which the system responds to the information that it has received. *Lead* illustrates the extent to which a system has the capacity to react to predictions about the future consequences of decisions and actions.

The relationship between these Deutsch describes in the following way: 'The chances of success in goal-seeking are . . . always related to the amounts of *load* and *lag*. Up to a point they may be positively related to the amount of *gain*, although, at high rates of gain, this relationship may be reversed; and they are always positively related to the amount of *lead*.'[17] At high rates of *gain* a system may over-respond to information received, and it is likely that above a certain rate of gain any increase will be dysfunctional to the realization of the system's goals.

It will be noticed that Deutsch lays much emphasis on the attainment of goals. In fact he refers to the 'similarity' of the processes of steering and goal seeking in living things *and* political systems. The analysis seems teleological and it may be wondered whether political systems, in particular, states, are organizations (in the sense of a business organization) and have definitive goals set for them. Deutsch makes the normal point that it is perhaps possible to set goals with respect to foreign affairs, but he only goes so far as to suggest that in addition to this, they 'may try to maintain some state of affairs they deem desirable, such as prosperity in economics or tranquillity in politics'.[18] It sometimes seems that Deutsch subsumes politics (with its multiplicity of often competing groups and goals) under government. He would, however, perhaps reply to this that conflicts of goals can be explained (and resolved eventually) in terms of blockages of channels and failures of signals to warn about the information load (its quantity, variety and disposition) within the system.[19]

We might note also that it is in terms of these concepts that Deutsch is able to define and thus, to some extent, to quantify or put values to, some of the traditionally intractable concepts of moral and political philosophy, like will and sovereignty. Thus *will* for example is defined as 'the putting into operation of data proposed from the past of a decision-making system in such a manner as to override most or all of the information currently received from its environment'.[20]

If we are to relate Deutsch's model to those which we have already described, we might say that he really tries to construct a model which combines an input-output type of analysis with that of an amended structural-functional analysis, for he sees it as possible for the original structural-functional model to incorporate notions like feedback, information flow and learning.[21] In this respect, then, there is a certain similarity between his communications model and that presented by Almond in his revised formulation.

CHAPTER VIII

Conclusion

We have been concerned in this section not so much to describe in all their completeness the models of political systems which our authors have attempted to construct, but to illustrate their major aspects, in order to show the assumptions that underlay the construction of the models: assumptions as much about scientific method as about the nature and purpose of politics and government. We attempt to make, now, a few remarks about these, by way of invoking some comparisons between our authors themselves.

There has been, first, general agreement among them that political systems must be viewed and analysed in systemic terms—as 'whole entities'. They emphasize that political systems must be analysed not simply 'systematically' but 'systemically'. As one writer puts it, 'the adjective which means "pertaining to system" is not "systematic" (which means something quite different) but systemic; and that is a word one seldom hears'.[1]

This idea that politics must be seen as a system is, they claim, a relatively new one, and it implies that the student of politics is capable of viewing the political system as a complete entity. It implies also, that political relations are constituted of interdependent parts, and that these relations cannot be viewed as 'discontinuous'. This is an assumption to which not all political scientists would adhere. The important point, however, and Easton is at pains to emphasize this, is that the concept of system is an *analytic* one, and does not necessarily imply an actually describable situation.

Secondly, our authors vary in the concern that they have, for analytical purposes, with the moral aspects of politics. While Almond makes reference to this, suggesting that his comparative analysis is 'relevant to the debates over the ethics and benefits of different types of political systems', and that capabilities analysis 'enables us to put such normative speculation on an empirical basis',[2] he cannot be said to make it an important part of his model. For Apter, on the other hand, this is a central theme of his scheme. Easton considers problems of this nature to be of the 'second order' type, and insists that whatever the character of the system, they are all composed of basic processes which should be the focus of comparison. Deutsch is close to Easton on this point; they both seem to suggest that the first duty of the political scientist is to provide a model showing why the political system is able to persist, and the processes and mechanisms by means of which it does so, and what are the conditions under which it can remain an efficient system. Problems about the 'proper' ends of the political system and governmental activity, are, from the point of view of analytical priorities, subsidiary to this. Similarly, in terms of the dynamic concept that they use, Easton's use of the notion of 'persistence' is much the same as Deutsch's employment of the notion of 'growth' of a political system.

Thirdly, with the possible exception of Apter, our authors insist that a scientific theory of politics must apply to politics in all its dimensions, and in all areas. There can be no special theory of the domestic political system that shows this system to be different in its essential variables, processes and functional requirements from politics in inter-state relations. The interpenetration of political systems, especially where such systems are not seen as bounded by geographical or geopolitical borders, means that the notion of political system is an analytical one, defined in terms of the problem which the scientist wishes to attempt to resolve. Political systems exist wherever 'political interactions' may be perceived; and political interactions may, and frequently do, transcend physical boundaries.

We can note, also, some other points which concern mainly some of the *assumptions* which underly the analyses and models of the authors dealt with here. Do we, for example, need to question Almond's assertion that an understanding of the processes of development of non-Western societies must be preceded by, and be based on, the tools of analysis and concepts derived from an understanding of Western 'modern' societies? Or, are these tools and concepts perhaps too general to allow us to make predictions about change and development in specific societies of varying cultures. Is there, in Almond's view here, an acceptance of the view of Marx, that 'the country that is more developed industrially only shows, to the less developed, the image of its own future'? [3]

We must also raise the problem of the extent to which, since the publication of *The Politics of the Developing Areas*, Almond has successfully been able to integrate the input-output method of analysis, characteristic of Easton's work, into the structural-functional framework that he has devised, with a view to alleviating the emphasis of that framework on stability.[4]

Finally, there is the suggestion that theoretical developments in the natural sciences, and developments in technology and in mathematics, have brought us to a situation in which it is possible to perceive important similarities, if not identities, in the behaviour of living things, electronic machines and social systems. The science of cybernetics for Deutsch, general systems theory for Easton, can now be used to analyse organizational behaviour in all these areas.

Deutsch has written that 'the analogies cybernetics may suggest between communication channels or control processes in machines, nerve systems, and human societies must in turn suggest new observations, experiments, or predictions that can be confirmed or refuted by the facts'.[5] An important implication of this analysis, for him, is that a theory of politics derived from cybernetic theory 'should link the "is" and the "ought" '.[6] This is a large claim, but it follows from the view that the aim of cybernetic analysis is *control* and exact prediction. Cybernetics is seen, as it were, as the bridge science between the natural and social sciences.

In somewhat similar terms, Easton has written that 'the perspectives of systems analysis serve to link all of the sciences natural and social'.[7] We have seen that Apter, for example, would not concur with the view that the methods of the natural sciences can simply be transferred for analysis in the social sciences. But as far as Deutsch and Easton are concerned at least, we may wonder, in the light of such statements, whether some modern political theorists would not look with general approval on the belief of Karl Marx, expressed in 1844, that 'natural science will one day incorporate the science of man, just as the science of man will incorporate natural science; there will be a *single* science'.[8]

PART THREE

*Typologies of
Political Systems*

CHAPTER IX

Introduction

Comparative politics is not an aspect of political science that has been discovered for the first time in the second half of the twentieth century. The comparison of political systems has been undertaken since the time when people first studied politics and political behaviour. Attempts to analyse actual political systems, and to classify them into relatively few broad types, and to discern patterns of development are as old and as varied as are the plethora of historical treatises concerned with political morality, with prescribing the ideal form of polity, and with setting out the rights and duties of ruled and ruler alike.

Yet, recent decades have seen important developments in this field. In the past, comparisons tended to be excessively formal; students concentrated primarily on the formal institutions of government, ignoring the all-important influence of informal social relationships in the process of deciding issues and in exercising political power. Insufficient attention was paid to the non-political forces that help to determine political behaviour and form the bases or context within which governmental institutions operate.

Furthermore, students of comparative politics since the mid-nineteenth century tended to deal only with countries of the Western world, that is, countries with similar cultural and socio-economic backgrounds. Representative democracy was taken as the ideal, whilst non-democratic systems and the undemocratic aspects of Western systems were regarded merely as deviations from this ideal.

In addition, students' treatment of the different systems

tended to be quite unsystematic. Their work is characterized by a dearth of orienting concepts and hypotheses designed to facilitate comparisons, and which can be tested against data collected systematically in various societies. Their work illustrates a concern with description rather than analysis. The country-by-country approach which they adopted prevented any truly comparative perspective being achieved. The similarities and uniformities of political behaviour and political relationships were not clearly revealed by this approach and testable hypotheses about political stability, change, revolutions, or development did not emerge.

Strictly speaking, these students[1] were more concerned with studying foreign governments than with comparative politics. Their efforts were directed to the collection of facts rather than to testing hypotheses about political behaviour *per se*. These shortcomings have been generally recognized by students of politics since the Second World War. This consensus has been produced by examples of parallel developments in cognate disciplines, notably cultural anthropology and sociology; and by the obvious inadequacy of traditional methods of study as a means of attaining an understanding of, in particular, the political systems of newly emergent nations, and in general, the increasing complexity of political life in the second half of the twentieth century.

The newly emerging nations have developed characteristics that make it impossible to treat all political systems as deviations, to a greater or lesser extent, from the democratic norm. Means have to be found to accommodate in our studies systems that are non-democratic, or culturally distinct, or economically underdeveloped, or exhibit only the formal institutional characteristics of a representative democracy. This cannot be done by using traditional approaches, that is, concentrating almost exclusively on such institutions as parliaments, executives, civil services, legal codes, etc. . . . This method is unlikely to yield particularly fruitful results or meaningful comparisons because institutions with the same name can and do perform vastly different roles in different political systems. Compare, for example, the role played by party in, say, Britain and the U.S.S.R. These are more accurately described as different institutions with the same name than as similar institutions that are comparable in terms of the functions they perform within their respective political systems. More important than the institutional, mechanistic arrangements of societies for the purpose of comparison and analysis are the non-institutionalized and non-political determinants of political behaviour such as the patterns of culture or the socio-economic arrangements within which the political system operates.

In recent decades the attentions of students of comparative politics have been concentrated in these directions. There has been a great increase in the scope of empirical work, especially in non-Western, under-developed areas; but, more important, there have been continuous efforts to gain the system and rigour that earlier studies lacked. This illustrates an aspect of the general concern among students of politics to adopt a more 'scientific' approach to their work. There have been, for example, innumerable attempts to provide 'models', hypotheses, and conceptual frameworks that enable the student to categorize all political systems, and facilitate the collection of data in a meaningful systematic fashion that allows comparison of the various systems as a whole or of selected aspects of them.

A major criticism to be made of contemporary developments in this field is that every student tends to be his own taxonomist. The number of classificatory schemes tends to increase as quickly as the number of empirical inquiries undertaken. The result is 'an almost embarrassing number of such schemes . . . requiring choices we do not really know how to make'.[2]

The concern to be rigorous and scientific has given rise to an almost incessant debate among scholars about the methodology of comparative politics, and the array of classificatory schemes exists primarily because there is a large degree of dissensus among them concerning the appropriate concepts, methods and analytical approaches specifically for the comparison of political

87

systems. The student approaching the subject for the first time has to choose between these various schemes. Before doing so he must address himself to such basic questions as the following: should one concentrate on formal organizations or on the informal processes of social and political life; should one base an analysis on structural categories or should functional categories only be used, or should a synthesis of both be attempted? Such questions can only be meaningfully answered in the context of one's immediate purposes, which delimit the kind of information one wishes to gather and the nature of the analysis one wishes to undertake. Different people have different purposes and interests which very often demand the use of different conceptual categories. Even so, differences of opinion exist among scholars concerning the applicability of particular categorizations in particular circumstances. This accounts in large measure for the protracted debates of recent years about methods and classifications.

Such debates, however, are an important and necessary part of the development of any scientific enterprise: that is, after the collection of data a period of reflection and evaluation of one's methods and conceptual tools is necessary. A great deal of information has been gathered about political behaviour, and a great many insights into its nature have been gained, from a number of perspectives. Hence a period of critical evaluation is necessary to disentangle the essential from the non-essential, the transient from the permanent, and the deliberate from the fortuitous. More important, it is a period in which the plethora of conceptual schemes can be considered and reconsidered, adapted, modified, or discarded as they are seen to be useful or otherwise. It is an opportunity for synthesizing the different schema so as to achieve a more comprehensive basis for analysis.

One of the ultimate aims and purposes of the present debate is to find a conceptual framework or frameworks that will enable political scientists to determine the place of such factors as political culture, ideology, historical development, and the whole range of forces that seek expression politically within the various kinds of political system. From this it is to be hoped that more general valid statements can be made about political behaviour as such. That such a framework is possible and likely to yield fruitful results is, at present, largely a matter of opinion and provides the *point d'appui* for much of the discourse in this field.

It is highly improbable, almost inconceivable, that any framework can be established that serves all analytical purposes at all times in all places. More likely is the possibility of establishing a classificatory scheme that facilitates the comparison and classification of political systems from a number of perspectives. Such a scheme would be in constant need of revision and modification as it is used to collect more and more data, and as the results it produces can be assessed in terms of the interests and purposes of political scientists. Progressively, therefore, the classifications will become more and more sophisticated and accurate, enabling the uniformities of political behaviour to be more clearly identified.

Thus the methodological debate taking place at present must not be seen as a temporary phenomenon likely to end in the near future never to reappear in the discussions of political scientists. It is, of necessity, a permanent feature of the development of a political *science*; but a feature which will assume different proportions and importance at different times, depending on the empirical work that has been done, is being done and is to be done, and on the agreement about the adequacy of current methods and concepts to meet the needs of analysts in an ever changing political system.

Meanwhile students of comparative politics have to select one (or more) of the many models to act as a basis for their empirical inquiries. Which they will chooose depends not only on their particular interests and the analytical categories most likely to yield the information they require, but also on their conceptions of the fundamental subject-matter of political science. For example, is the political system best analysed as an autonomous system or as a subsystem of the social system? To which aspect of its social environment is political behaviour best related? Should it be analysed with reference to, for example, the cultural background, personality structure, or to the level of economic development? Different answers to questions such as these are partly the result of the different interests of political scientists, and partly the result of their different conceptions of their subject. Such variations help explain the proliferation of classificatory schemes in recent years. Which of these schemes will be favoured by any particular political scientist at any particular time will depend on the kind of comparison he wishes to make, on the type of problem to which he is addressing himself.

The present concentration on taxonomy and lengthy methodological treatises is, therefore, not a sign of the infancy of political science *per se*, but of the increasing awareness among political scientists of the need for rigour and system if their energies are to be adequately rewarded. Unlike students of previous generations they find it necessary to return to the fundamentals of their subject, making clear the myriad assumptions on which their endeavours are based, and outlining in great detail the conceptual edifices they have erected on these assumptions, and which they intend to use in furthering the development of their discipline. The main problem for the new student of comparative politics today is not a dearth of ideas but the sheer variety of approaches to his field.

Most of the typologies of political systems that have appeared in recent years are based on conceptions borrowed and adapted from other disciplines, such as anthropology, economics and physics. The remainder of this section describes some of these. They were selected primarily not because they possess qualities of excellence that are not to be found in the works of any other scholars, nor because they appear to the present authors to provide insights into the nature of political systems over and above other taxonomies; rather they were selected because they are among the most well known of recent typologies, because they present fairly lucid, clear 'types' for differentiating political systems, and because they, in combination, illustrate clearly the heterogeneous sources from which current concepts in comparative politics are drawn.

It is not our intention to make a critical evaluation of the various schema. Similarly no synthesis of these conceptions is attempted. This is perhaps one of the more pressing needs at the present time, but is a task that is best left to those who have first attempted to apply a number of these schemes co-terminously.

CHAPTER X

E. A. Shils and Modernization

Political institutions change and political values change. In some societies considerable changes in institutions and values take place speedily by means of revolution. In other societies change takes place in a smooth evolutionary way involving little civil disturbance or the use of force of an overt sort. Between these extremes lie many gradations of political and social stability and instability. To measure such gradations is a major goal of social and political research.

There are innumerable ways in which the phenomenon of change can be incorporated into one's analysis. For example, philosophers of history sometimes present us with grand pictures of the transcendental nature of the development of society and of the state, whilst economists and sociologists concern themselves at a less lofty level with the difficulties of dynamic analysis. What emerges from all such attempts to analyse this phenomenon is that political change is intricately related to a wide spectrum of social and economic factors. For example, the institution of government-sponsored schemes of public education, or of welfare services, may contribute to new demands being made on the political system which, in turn, may lead to the appearance of a social movement which may ultimately necessitate political changes of a far-reaching nature. Witness the advent of democratic forms and the growth of the welfare state in Britain.

Political change to be understood in its widest context must therefore be related to many aspects of social life, study of which must properly fall outside of the competence of the political scientist. It must be seen in the context of such interrelated factors as industrialization, urbanization, technological developments, education, commerce, cultural and sociological developments, and communications networks. The ultimate objective must be to construct a scheme that incorporates these factors in a comprehensive analysis of social change. This, however, cannot be achieved without a vast amount of empirical and conceptual analysis being undertaken at lower levels of generality.

Political development when considered in isolation from other aspects of social development tends to be equated with change in certain prescribed directions. There are a number of reasons why such associations are not altogether unacceptable. Concern with change thus comes to have positive humanitarian connotations, displaying a concern with the general improvement in the human condition towards certain prescribed standards. Furthermore, such notions are usually contemplated as correlatives of economic development and social development, which can be gauged in terms of productivity, levels of capital investment, literacy, birth and infant-mortality rates and consumption patterns. Thus the notion of political improvement facilitates the more inclusive object of assessing the multifarious aspects of social development generally.

It is probable that, with hindsight, the most important political innovation of the twentieth century will be identified as the ending of the colonial-imperialist era and the emergence, sometimes as newly independent states, of the nations of Latin America, Asia, Africa and the Middle East. It is extremely difficult to find an adequate means of describing these countries collectively, but in the absence of better alternatives we have chosen the term 'developing',[1] whilst recognizing that, in spite of its humanitarian connotations, it does not adequately identify the diversities in location, population, history, culture, religion and resources which characterize such widely different countries as India, Ghana, Mexico, Iran or Thailand.

Despite their differences all these countries are involved in more than the usual process of continuous change that is a characteristic of every society. Every one of these (and many others besides) are involved in change that is critical, disruptive and consciously sought. All are in a process of transition from the traditional agrarian type of politico-economic structures to a modern style of life. The transition is such that these nations can no longer be described as traditional nor yet have they achieved modernity.

There is a degree of agreement within these 'developing' nations not only on the general direction of change but on the actual objectives sought. For example, Edward Shils in his *Political Development in the New States* postulates as a universal aspiration among contemporary states the desire to be free of 'dependence on the West'.[2] More positively their goal is to be modern, that is, 'dynamic, concerned with the people, democratic and equalitarian, scientific, economically advanced, sovereign and influential. The model of modernity adopted by newly emergent states is that of '. . . the West detached in some way from its geographical origins and locus'.[3]

The new states in which these aspirations are most pronounced and most urgently sought exist mainly in Asia and Africa. They have certain characteristics which help to distinguish them as a group. For example,

1. They have recently acquired independence following a substantial period of foreign-Western rule; therefore their indigenous machinery of government is of quite recent origin.
2. Their social structures and cultures are on the whole highly traditional.
3. Significant sections of their elite are concerned to modernize their social structure, their culture, and their political life and outlook.

This desire to be modern places great stress on the resources of these countries and strains the aspirations of the elites considerably. Many obstacles stand in the way of modernization, all of which have to be overcome before any substantial progress can be made towards the realization of a Western style polity. The

inherited body of traditional beliefs, the existing social structure, the scarcity of the human material of politics, and the
moral and intellectual qualities of the elites themselves all affect
the operation of the political system, revealing its true potentialities and thus affecting the nature of the ideal sought as well as
the means of attaining it. The political systems of the new states
are invariably subject to the dichotomous pull of traditionality
on the one hand and modernity on the other.

SOCIAL STRUCTURE

The social structure is one of the factors which affects political
development in all countries, but is of particular importance in
the newly emergent states because of the immensity of the gap
between the ideal and the actual. In most of these states some
form of kinship system exists. It may manifest itself through loyalties to a caste or through strong affiliations to linguistic
groups. Such schismatic factors tend to alienate many individuals and groups from the system at large, preventing them
from participating in the political processes of their societies.
Their loyalties are confined to narrow, locally circumscribed
objects, which result in inward looking attitudes inimical to the
emergence of political modernity. For example, such parochial
loyalties make it difficult to achieve the rule of law, and because
of the tendency to favour kinsmen, caste-fellows and co-
believers it is difficult to attain justice in administration and
adjudication.

One of the main characteristics of industrialized, urbanized
societies is the size and structure of their middle, professional
classes, many of whose members possess the necessary qualities
and characteristics to enable them to play a leading part in the
economic and commercial life of these societies. From their
ranks are drawn the bureaucrats, executives and administrators,
innovators who maintain the dynamism of the system and who
adjust patterns of production to the ever-changing patterns of
consumption. This section of society is functionally of particular
importance because they, to a greater extent than any other

group, have internalized the norms of rational calculation, as well as being more firmly committed to using scientific methods to solve the problems confronting society. The norms, attitudes and methods of these classes are important because they are the norms, attitudes and methods which have supported the social, economic and political life of modern complex Westernized societies. The developing states, by contrast, have little or no middle class to perform these functions. They contain many small traders who might be regarded as the forerunners of the modern executive, but they are largely illiterate, with no great assimilation of modern culture, and possessing very few modern economic skills.

In all societies differentials in the range, scope and levels of educational attainment tend to distinguish the habits, tastes, interests and recreational activities of some members and groups from others. In Western states, however, education for all to a prescribed minimum level is provided; and even those who pursue their studies to an advanced level are educated in the same language with the same basic value patterns and manipulate a common core of basic symbols with their less accomplished neighbours. In the new states, however, the vast majority of the population is almost completely without formal education. Consequently, the possession of a higher education not only enhances claims to respect from one's fellow men, but also creates wide divergences between the educated and uneducated sections of society with respect to such things as habits of dress, recreations, tastes in food and drink as well as in their assessments of what is of value in life and which goals ought to be given priority.

In general the new states possess agricultural economies, using the most traditional methods and techniques, which result in a comparatively low *per capita* income in these societies. Overcoming this is seen by the majority of governments in these areas as the major problem of reconstruction and reform. The elites of the new states are, almost invariably, in favour of economic development, striving incessantly to realize and develop better resources, increased efficiency and the accumulation of capital. Such developments will not only raise the standards of living in society but will also provide a useful basis from which to gain a hearing and become politically and socially significant in the world.

Almost without exception among Western states institutional arrangements are such that decision makers are either elected by the people at large or are legally answerable to, and act on behalf of, those who are representative of the people. In this sense the predominant characteristic of authoritative decisions in these states is that they are democratically based. There are, inevitably, many non-democratic institutionalized features which affect the decision making process. For example, the hierarchical nature of party organization in which the power of initiative usually lies at the top rather than spontaneously rising from below. Nevertheless the general degree of commitment to democratic forms is great, and the corresponding feelings of involvement in social and political affairs among the population make it unlikely that decisions will for very long go unchallenged.

Authority in the new states however tends to be far more hierarchically structured. The traditional orientations of these societies remove many issues from the realm of the decision makers. Traditional responses, customs and rituals still carry the authority which they have always done. Even where decisions are necessary, little attempt is made to involve the population at large. The right to participate in deciding, both in the institutions of government and in the limited number of voluntary associations, is largely confined to members of particular kinship and lineage groups, or to those belonging to religious or caste communities. This hierarchical structure of authority results in either excessive submissiveness among the people at large, or adherence to extremist egalitarian ideals as a reaction against the established system.

The universal aspiration to modernity clearly involves the political scientist in broadening the focus of his analysis and in developing new concepts and methods with which to achieve an understanding of these aspirations as they manifest themselves in the real world. Men have always been guided in their political activities by ideals and visions of the type of society they wish to achieve. Never before, however, has the ideal gained such universal expression, nor has it been reflected to such a high degree among other nations, as has the ideal of a modern, industrialized, mass society among the developing nations today. The elites of the new states today have, as it were, operationalized versions of their goals constantly before them. The ideals sought by the new states are, therefore, in general, very similar. Shils summarizes these as 'a regime of *civilian rule* through *representative institutions* in the matrix of *public liberties*'.[4] Comparisons and contrasts of these new states can therefore be based on such factors as:

    1. How far they deviate from this 'model' of democracy.
    2. At what speed they wish to approach their ideal.
    3. How, in practice, they combine oligarchic with democratic tendencies, or modernizing aspirations with traditional loyalties, etc. . . .

Shils postulates five models of modernizing nations which purport to characterize the various responses to the problems encountered by the new states. His discussions, especially of political democracy and totalitarian oligarchy, are such, however, that this typology facilitates the comparison, not only of the emergent nations, but of most political systems in the modern world. Each of his models will now be described in some detail.

POLITICAL DEMOCRACY

By political democracy Shils refers to the system towards which, he says, modernizing nations, by and large, strive. He defines it as a 'regime of civilian rule through representative institutions and public liberties'.[5] The focal point of such a system is a legislative body which is periodically elected by universal suffrage.

The power to initiate legislation lies with this body and may be exercised either through its own individual members or through committees, or through executive leadership which may be separately elected (as in the U.S.A.) or selected from members of the legislature (as in G.B.). Legislatively this assembly is supreme, it has the right to accept or to reject any proposals put to it by the executive, and no bill can become law without its consent. Its time is spent largely in debate, questioning members of the executive and reviewing budgetary provisions, by which it is enabled to control and scrutinize the work of the executive. Policies are carried out by a hierarchically organized bureaucracy which is answerable to the legislature through the member of the executive who has been appointed its political head.

Political parties are an integral feature of these systems. Those seeking election usually do so as members of one of the contending parties, and the party which succeeds in winning the largest number of seats dominates the legislature, and the executive (where the British example is followed) is drawn from its ranks or from the ranks of a coalition of parties who in conjunction command a majority of the elected assembly. Where the executive is elected separately the successful candidate is expected to work with the majority party in the legislature.

Another feature of these systems is that political power is held for a comparatively short period of time, and the conditions for maintaining it are fairly precisely defined. Periodically the electorate is given the opportunity to choose anew between the contending groups striving for political office. In order that such a choice be meaningful it is necessary that a relatively high degree of freedom of discussion and comment should be allowed. Continuous scrutiny and criticism of political decisions by a free press and the other organs of public opinion must be permitted for the competition for political leadership to have any significance. Similarly, within the legislature the activities of the government must be subject to scrutiny and criticism by members of the minority, opposition parties, and also by the back-bench members of the governing party.

Any tendency towards the tyrannical and arbitrary abuse of power is thus curbed by the ability to keep politics in the open so that it may be the object of scrutiny. The continuing confidence and support of the legislative assembly and the electorate are the necessary conditions for the maintenance of political power. The loss of either, registered by an adverse vote on a major issue in the assembly or an electoral defeat at the polls, requires that power be relinquished, and that machinery be set in motion for placing it in the hands of those who hold the confidence of society.

Two further characteristics of these regimes are the existence of an independent judiciary, and the recognition by all political actors that their conduct must be circumscribed by the provisions of the constitutional, conventional and legal limitations of their society. The former must be capable of protecting the rights of citizens against the extralegal encroachments of the state and of regulating relationships between citizens.

For political democracy to be effective and stable these institutional arrangements must be supported by certain social and cultural preconditions. Participants must display a willingness and desire to operate within the established institutional system. They must exercise what Schumpeter has called 'democratic self-control'.[6] Every opportunity to embarrass and overthrow the government must not be seized upon by the opposition, who, like their counterparts in the government, must be prepared to exercise a certain amount of 'give and take' on non-essential matters, whilst maintaining the full force of their opposition for the vital matters of political principle which distinguish their belief systems from those of their opponents.

For any system of politics to be stable it must necessarily have the continued acceptance by society at large of the authority of the government of the day. To a large extent this depends on its ability to effectively promulgate and execute policy, which in turn depends on what Shils calls 'the stability, coherence and effectiveness of the ruling elite'.[7] The institution of political parties facilitates this condition. They enable working relationships between the leadership and the party rank and file both in parliament and in the country to be established. Members are held to the party partly by the expectation of seeing policies of which they approve enacted, and partly by the expectation that their chances of electoral victory will be enhanced. On the other hand a major factor determining the electoral and parliamentary support accorded to leaders is the extent to which they can incorporate within their programmes the various demands of the numerous minority groups in society and in the party.

In addition to the coherence of intra-party relationships it is necessary that political leaders should be attached to representative institutions as such. There must be a genuine desire to make them work, and a willingness to accord the opposition its rights and liberties at all times. There must be a degree of 'mutual regard and solidarity' among political leaders, which at times may require a 'closing of ranks' by moderates to prevent extremists from gaining the ascendancy.

There must also be an adequately trained and organized civil service to carry out the decisions of the politicians. Of necessity it must be politically unaligned, ready to serve any duly constituted government, and sufficiently independent to offer strong, objective advice on the political problems of the day to incumbent ministers.

These, together with adequate police and security forces and a general commitment to the values underlying the democratic method, constitute the most important features of a political democracy. No society fulfils all the conditions for the operation of a successful and stable democracy, but in many states, primarily in the West but including also, for example, India and Japan these conditions are sufficiently approximated to enable them to be subsumed under the title of political democracy.

TUTELARY DEMOCRACY

The institutional arrangements of political democracy are only meaningful when operating in appropriate circumstances, that is, where there is a general commitment to the norms and values of political democracy, where political allegiances are firm but not all-embracing. Sophisticated political attitudes, which are a necessary correlate of political democracy, tend to develop only among those whose lives are economically and materially secure, which has only been achieved nationally in modernized, industrialized societies.

Consequently, in many societies, attitudes emerge even among those who are ideologically committed to the development of a political democracy, that it may be desirable to modify their short-term goals by restructuring the polity so that effective, stable government may be achieved quickly in order to modernize the economy and society, and thus develop the propensity of the citizenry to participate in political democracy. Often this entails reducing the power of the legislature and of the political parties, thus enhancing executive power, whilst retaining the safeguards of the rule of law and public liberties. Representative institutions and the institutions of public opinion would be maintained but their powers would be severely limited in scope; thus maintaining the institutional framework of political democracy, whilst the power of initiative lies almost completely with the executive.

This variant of political democracy appeals to the elites of new states because it affords an authoritative system in societies whose institutions of public opinion and civil orders are incapable of fulfilling the roles demanded of them in political democracy, whilst maintaining the political structures which can be utilized meaningfully as the propensities of these societies for doing so develop. Tutelary democracy is thus the result of a kind of pragmatic response by committed democrats to situations which seem to be inherently incapable of effectively operating democratic institutions. As such, it is not the institutionalization of a theory or political doctrine.

Institutionally, political democracy is maintained, but in operation, it is modified to give greater power to the executive.

Discipline, and thus authority, is maintained by a strong personality, or a group of strong personalities at the centre, controlling both the dominant political party and the state. Often this is achieved by a fusion of the roles of party leader and head of state. Parliament's influence is reduced considerably by a variety of means. Although maintaining the right to discuss, inquire and ratify, it is rendered less effective by the overt discouragement of the executive, the domination of the party and the curtailment of the opposition. Often the freedom of the press and of the universities to comment and criticize is curtailed, or held conditional upon a judicious use of their freedom.

The successful operation of tutelary democracy depends to a very large extent on the sincerity of the elite's attachment to the development of political democracy, on its willingness to allow the effective operation of established institutional forms, and to reduce its own power as the capacity of the society to operate democratically grows stronger. Indications of its sincerity in these matters are given by the extent to which it uses coercion for political purposes, the degree of mutual trust existent between members of the executive, and the relationship it establishes with those agencies of opposition that are entitled to operate under the law. Even in the most difficult of circumstances the idea of a legitimate opposition must be maintained. Opportunities must be provided for friendly contact to take place between the executive and their political opponents so that at the very least some notion of informal influence is created.

As with political democracy, tutelary democracy requires the services of a competent, loyal bureaucracy capable of providing dispassionate and informed criticisms of projected policies. In tutelary democracies, however, this critical role is all the more important because of the weakness of parliamentary criticism of executive policy.

MODERNIZING OLIGARCHIES
Tutelary democratic regimes emerge as a result of the recognition of the wide gap which exists, especially in the new states,

between the sophisticated demands of the polity and the apathy, parochialism and general indifference exhibited in society. Tutelary democrats, however, are not discouraged by this gap, but see the emergent regime as merely an interim measure which will give way to fully developed political democracy as soon as the sociopolitical norms of the citizenry develop appropriately. This is an essentially optimistic view of the human material of politics, based on the belief that the apathetic and parochial individual of today can develop the traits and attitudes of the responsible citizen of a sophisticated political democracy.

Other observers, however, are less optimistic in this direction. They interpret the 'gap' as a constant attribute of political life, at least for the foreseeable future. Furthermore, they see it as a factor that is likely to reduce drastically, if not nullify, the society's chances of achieving the necessary degree of social and economic modernity to develop politically. Often the response of those with such views is to turn away from a democratically based polity to a more authoritarian regime which they believe can deliver the type of society they seek quickly and efficiently by providing a government which is strong, stable, and honest: that is, a modernizing oligarchy.

Such regimes may be drawn either from the civilian or the military spheres. In both cases the elite must be well organized, with membership relatively restricted and close scrutiny made of all aspirants to membership. Civilian oligarchies must maintain close control over the military to prevent subversion of its position by the latter. Military regimes, however, because of their superior position *vis-à-vis* physical force, and because of their need to gain the co-operation of influential leaders in society may be more or less conciliatory towards the civilian elites.

Parliament in modernizing oligarchies is stripped of all its traditional powers. It has no power to propose, debate, or revise legislation; nor does it provide the forum from which an alternative government will emerge. Parliament is reduced to an acclamatory institution with merely a ratifying role. No opposition is allowed. This is achieved in a number of ways which can be more or less legal, more or less covert. For example, all, or all but one of the political parties could be dissolved; election results could be tampered with; or leaders and/or supporters of opposition parties could be persecuted, murdered, or imprisoned.

The goal of modernization necessitates efficient machinery of bureaucratic administration, and in many cases this involves relying on the established civil service existent before the oligarchical elites came to power. Military elites will invariably keep the old personnel whilst placing their own supporters in key positions. Civilian elites may be even more dependent, calling on many experienced civil servants to assume cabinet office.

For a number of reasons, the traditional machinery and practices for promoting justice are subverted in modernizing oligarchies. An independent judiciary enforcing the rule of law is symptomatic of the old democratic methods which are slow and cumbersome, and therefore contrary to the needs of the elite who wish to make decisive incursions on the road to modernity. Formal justice, in the traditional Western sense, may hamper their progress, and thus allegiance tends to be given to the notion of natural justice appertaining to the momentary situation rather than to justice in the sense of applying formally prescribed rules. Furthermore, oligarchical regimes are usually intent on dissociating themselves from their predecessors. A convenient way of doing this is to stage a number of 'treason trials' involving former leaders and 'personal symbols of a period of national degradation'.[8] The traditional machinery of justice is unsuitable for these purposes.

Because such regimes are so unrepresentative in character (that is, unrepresentative in the formal democratic sense) they tend to evoke a great deal of antagonism and opposition. Opposition, however, has to be of a clandestine nature because of the prohibitive tendencies of the regime. Elites, in order to avoid conspiracy and subversion and to maintain stability, must, in these circumstances, rely heavily on the police and the army, whose personnel tend to be more evident in political life than they are in more liberal regimes.

TOTALITARIAN OLIGARCHY

A common feature of the political systems of both tutelary democracy and modernizing oligarchies is that they are both fairly simple responses to a given situation. They differ only in the interpretation made by the elites of the potentialities of the society for developing and sustaining the necessary degree of political, intellectual and technological ability to realize the modernity which they seek. Both systems are merely pragmatic responses to the needs of the emergent situation, and not motivated by some highly articulated body of doctrine. Their dealings with and attitudes towards the numerous social institutions of varying political significance can be relatively flexible. They can establish working relationships with any parliamentary opposition, with the press, the universities, business, etc. . . . , based on existing circumstances and common interest rather than in accordance with preconceived axioms of 'right' relationships.

Totalitarian oligarchy is different from both of these systems in so far as it is guided by a political doctrine. In this century the two most important doctrines of totalitarianism have been communism of the Left and fascism of the Right. One of the defining features of totalitarian oligarchy is the belief that the ruling clique (based on class, race or some other feature agreed on by the elite) possess knowledge of the 'good life' and of the means of achieving it, which because of their historic mission is denied to others in society. Their role is therefore seen as that of catalysts of historical processes and procurers of that which the people would have if only they knew their 'true' interests. By such arguments as these, totalitarian oligarchy surrounds itself with claims of being truly democratic as opposed to the sham democracies in the liberal tradition.

Another feature of totalitarianism which follows from its

predilection towards an official ideology is the belief in the superiority of the polity in all social matters. It admits of no independent centre of power, and seeks to dominate all spheres of life. Therefore, unlike modernizing oligarchies, totalitarian oligarchies cannot actively seek working relationships and compromises with rival centres of power, like religious communities, business interests or landowners. In practice, compromises do emerge but they are symptomatic of failure on the part of the regime to win over or to coerce members of these groups. The compromise is not the result of a confluence of wills so much as an expedient arrangement concluded by a defeated, recalcitrant state.

The elite in a totalitarian oligarchy is a highly disciplined and coherent body, bound together by its doctrine through the institution of the party. The party is the essential organ through which the elite conducts its operations. More precisely the party establishes a bureaucracy of its own which controls the party structure at its various levels of existence and which also controls through the party the state bureaucracy. The party possesses a monopoly of power and tolerates the existence of no other party. In the case of Communism, this is associated with the Marxian view that parties are manifestations of class interests and that a multiplicity of parties merely reflects a multiplicity of classes, each striving to realize its interests, if necessary, at the expense of others. Where a proletarian party is in the ascendant it is argued that the need for more than one party disappears, since inevitably, all classes other than the proletariat have, or are about to, disappear.

Totalitarian oligarchy maintains parliamentary institutions for propagandist and ceremonial purposes only; they have no powers to initiate or revise. Both of these functions are performed by the very small group who constitute the executive committee of the party. Similarly, institutions involving the participation of the citizen body are maintained only for acclamatory purposes. Elections, for example, do not determine the composition of the elite—not even in the very limited sense in which elections in, say Britain or the U.S.A., determine which of two or more sets of competing leaders shall hold political office at any particular time. Furthermore, they have no more than a minimal influence on the direction of policy.

In this type of regime, as with modernizing oligarchies, the rule of law, an independent judiciary, and a legally constituted opposition are dispensed with. The elite of the party are the ultimate arbiters in all legal matters of any political significance. Similarly, public opinion as an expression of judgments on policies is disallowed. Instead, an intelligentsia seeking to defend and justify all decisions of the party is fostered. In this way, the synthetic atmosphere of consensus that surrounds politics in these states is produced.

TRADITIONAL OLIGARCHY

One of the most important foci for comparative purposes in politics is the public bureaucracy. This is so in spite of the fact that many leading political scientists at the present time show a preference for a functional or non-structural approach. This, however, is not to argue that a functional approach to the comparative study of political systems is inferior to a structural approach; rather it is believed that the public bureaucracy in particular offers a promising basis for comparison and avoids any of the conceptual difficulties involved in locating a given function, say, 'rule application', through a multitude of structures. One must of course be aware of the basic dangers pointed out by the functionalists that structures may vary considerably from system to system, and that similar structures in different systems may have significant functional differences that can easily be overlooked. These difficulties, however, need not necessarily vitiate the exercise of singling out one structure or set of structures and analysing the functions it performs. It can be especially useful in the case of the public bureaucracy which is a common feature of all modern nation states. Equally though, it must be recognized that while these difficulties cause few problems when Western states are being studied because there is a high degree of correlation of the various structures and the corresponding functions in the different systems, there are more difficulties involved with developing countries. A structural basis of comparison is feasible if the institution or institutions actually exist in corresponding form in the political systems under study, and if notice is taken of variations in the functional role of institutions in different systems. In developing countries it is the absence or precarious existence of comparable institutions that complicates comparison of their political systems.

The recent imperial experience of most new states has resulted in a dearth of large scale bureaucratic structures operated by traditional oligarchies. Control of administration, as of most other sectors of social life, was kept in the hands of the imperial power, and traditional elites consequently became politically impotent and ineffective. In the emergent situation the desire for modernity and a centralized interventionist state outweighs the not inconsiderable sympathy which still exists for the traditional style of life and culture. Traditional governmental structures are therefore advocated as the long-term institutional arrangements of the polity by only a very few of those active participants in the public life of the new states.

Traditional oligarchy is, therefore, not, as such, a viable alternative form for political development, but at any one time traces of traditional oligarchy will be found operating in political life. Absolute change can never be achieved in either the social or political spheres; thus, even in the most determinedly modernizing nations, traditional customs, outlooks, structures, and culture will infuse the emerging situation with their influence. Although at the level of conscious, rational and deliberate choice preponderance will be given to the techniques and demands of modernization, subconscious, non-rational and involuntary responses will still orient behaviour around traditional patterns involving to a large extent traditional oligarchies.

Traditional oligarchy is based on a strong dynastic constitution associated with traditional religious beliefs. Rulers emerge on the basis of kinship alone or by a combination of kinship and selection by persons qualified by kinship to participate in the selection process. The ruler's counsellors and immediate confidants form a palace retinue chosen by the ruler on the basis of kinship or personal choice.

No legislative body is deemed necessary because of the minute amount of new legislation, which, when needed, is initiated and executed by the ruler and his advisors. For similar reasons bureaucratic machinery in this type of regime is almost unknown. Traditional oligarchy provides few services beyond the basic minimum, and interferes as little as possible in the social and economic life of the community. The civil service, in so far as such an institution exists at all, is of very limited size and is recruited as part of the ruler's household retinue, rather than as a piece of bureaucratic apparatus in the modern sense.

Unlike regimes more fully committed to modernization traditional oligarchy is ill-equipped to intervene actively; partly because it lacks any cohesive machinery of control and order. The rudimentary organization of the army and the police facilitates control of sporadic outbursts by small dissident groups and vociferous individuals only.

The central government is never strong. Consequently localities, composed of kinship groups or territorial units, tend to amass a great deal of power which is exercised independently of the central government. Often, structures appear which are reminiscent of the feudal arrangements of France in the ninth century, or Germany in the twelfth, where local magnates maintained their own monetary systems as well as their own machinery for order and justice.

Social organization is so rudimentary that the public tends to be uninformed about public matters. No institutions for the dissemination of knowledge or the creation of public opinion exists. Consequently, 'public opinion, in the sense of legitimate, openly critical, discussion of governmental action and inaction, is absent'.[9]

Such regimes as these tend to be resolutely opposed to the

aspirations of modernity, and seek legitimacy on the grounds that they are protecting the traditional culture. Although, in spite of these claims, very often what is achieved in practice is an erosion of the traditional culture and structure of government which is replaced by an oligarchical constitution.

*   *   *

The foregoing descriptions of types of political regime outline some of the characteristics which actual political systems may develop in their attempts, which may be more or less consciously made, to achieve modernity. None of the alternatives have been, or are likely to be, fully realized as they have been described or as they are conceived by their various proponents. Such is the nature of political ideals. Which course will be pursued, which ideal will be sought depends on the particular circumstances on particular occasions as well as on the predilections and perceptions of those most influential politically in society. To what extent the political ideal will be realized depends on a number of factors, the most important of which is perhaps the capacity of the elite for self-restraint and to deliver the goods of modernity to which it has pledged itself. The ease of transition from traditionality to modernity in all spheres of social life depends to a great extent initially on the elite's ability to establish a working compromise with the claims of traditional beliefs, and through time, on their ability to 'reinterpret traditional beliefs, adapt them to modern needs and translate them into the modern idiom'.[10]

CHAPTER XI

G. A. Almond and
Political Culture

Almond attempts to construct a scheme for the methodical comparison of political systems by adapting concepts borrowed from the fields of sociology and anthropology. In this way, he believes, the major political systems which exist in the world today can be classified according to a common set of categories. He starts from the view that a political system is a system of action about which there is no difficulty in gaining information, that is political activity is empirically observable behaviour.

In the past, attempts to compare political systems have concentrated on their legal-institutional aspects. This approach, Almond argues, will not result in any meaningful comparisons of actual systems, but comparisons only of their legal frameworks. In addition to the formal institutions of government, the student of politics must take into account the parts played by family ties, mobs, electorates, casual and persistent groupings, and all foci of power and influence in the political process, if his analysis is to be directly relevant to political systems as they are.

The result is that Almond classifies political systems on the basis of their *structures* and *cultures*. These two concepts are so intricately related that it is impossible to discuss either in isolation; the political culture of a society is greatly affected by the political structure, while the operation of the structure is conditioned by the cultural context in which it is set.

To elucidate the relationship between the two, Almond introduces the further concepts of *roles* and *orientations to political action*. He sees all political activities in terms of fulfilling roles. An individual's political activities become relevant for the student of political systems not only for what he does or says, but also for the reasons he gives for doing them, and the significance attached to those activities by other persons. In complex political systems such as exist today, political activities are governed not only by the inclinations and capabilities of individuals and groups, but also by the ideas these people hold about the system as a whole and of their part in it. In other words the political system is seen as a set of interactive roles, or a structure of roles. Each political actor (an individual or a group) fulfils a role and his activities are delimited and directed by his conception of the role, and his understanding of what others within the system expect of him as a role incumbent. Each actor fulfils a number of roles, which are sometimes complementary to each other, but which can conflict with each other in terms of the norms and expectations which are invariably attached to political roles. Thus, the same person may fill the roles of prime minister and party leader. For the most part his activities can combine successfully the norms and expectations attached to both offices; although sometimes he must distinguish carefully between the two roles and relate his activities to one of them only. This can be seen in operation when, for example, the P.M. appears on television to make *either* a party political broadcast *or* a speech to the nation as leader of the government. Such role differentiation is practised more in some societies than in others, and this is one of the most important criteria adopted by Almond in his classificatory scheme of political systems.

Political systems operate within the framework of a set of meanings and purposes, which are described by Almond as the political culture of a society. This is another important factor in his classification of the political systems of the modern world. He outlines three basic 'models' of political culture which characterize the various attitudes towards political activity found among individuals in different societies. These models are like

Weber's ideal types—they characterize certain aspects of empirical political systems, but do not reflect precisely those systems. There is no necessary relationship between any one model of a political culture and any one political system. Consequently, 'the United States, England, and several of the Commonwealth countries have a common political culture, but are separate and different kinds of political system'.[1]

The concept of political culture is an attempt to find one rubric to include what, in the past, have been variously described as attitudes to politics, political values, ideologies, national character, and cultural ethos, etc. . . . . None of these terms is sufficiently broad to provide a basis for classifying political systems, each one of them separately is relevant to the study of comparative politics, but each one is vague and ambiguous and, as such, serves only as a source of confusion for those attempting to compare political systems methodically. The concept of political culture is an attempt to gain the rigour and comprehensiveness which these other concepts lack.

Political cultures are measured in terms of 'orientation to political action', which refers to the knowledge the individual has of political objects, events, actions and issues; whether or not he invests them with any emotional significance; how he evaluates them; and whether he is sufficiently stirred to action by them. Political culture is thus the pattern of orientations to political action within any given society.

To establish the precise pattern of an individual's general orientation to politics, information must be gathered about his knowledge of, involvement with, and judgment on each of four main objects of political orientation. These are:

First, the system as a whole. What is his knowledge of, feelings for, and judgments on the history, size, location, power and constitutional characteristics of his nation and its political system?

Second, the input process, organized around the institutions which channel the flow of demands made by society on the political system, and which initiate the conversion of these demands into authoritative policies. These include political parties, interest groups and the media of mass communication. Information must be sought about an individual's knowledge, feelings and opinions of the structures and roles of the groups which are influential in political life, and of the specific policy proposals which they make.

Third, the output process, which includes the work of the bureaucracy and the courts and other institutions concerned with applying and enforcing authoritative decisions. What knowledge does the individual possess of policy enforcement, and of the structures involved with it? Does he have any strong feelings about them? What are his judgments on them?

Fourth, the self. What part does he see himself playing in the political system? What is his knowledge of his rights, powers, and obligations? Does he know how to gain access to influential persons or groups, or how to maximize his own influence? And, what criteria does he use in forming opinions of the system and his place within it?

The political culture of a society is determined by correlating information about these aspects collected from a valid sample of the population. That is, the political culture is determined by '. . . the frequency of different kinds of cognitive, affective and evaluative orientations towards the political system in general, its input and output aspects, and the self as political actor'.[2]

TYPES OF POLITICAL CULTURE

On the basis of such considerations, Almond argues, three distinct types of political culture can be discerned. They are the parochial, subject, and participant cultures respectively. In pure form, the *parochial political culture* exists only in simple traditional societies in which there is very little specialization, and where actors fulfil a combination of political, economic, and religious roles simultaneously. There are therefore no specialized political roles. This means that the chieftain in tribal society fulfils at one and the same time political, religious and economic roles and any specific action is not consciously related to any one of these roles (if it is consciously related to the idea of fulfilling roles at all).

The orientations of the individual in a parochial culture tend to follow the pattern of the undifferentiated role structure. They tend to be political-cum-economic-cum-religious orientations, in so far as they exist at all. In such a culture the individual tends not to be aware of the system as such. His orientations to the four specialized political objects are, in general, negative. That is, he is unaffected by the agencies of central government; they hardly encroach upon his consciousness.[3] Consequently, he tends to be aware of the structures and operations of his local community only. In terms of the total political system he is not oriented to political action at all. Since he is not aware of the existence of the total system he therefore has no feelings about or opinions on it.

Such an extreme situation rarely exists, however. Far more likely is the situation in which the individual is aware of the existence of the central political authority, but his feelings for and evaluation of the system have not crystallized sufficiently for him to establish for himself norms and standards to regulate his relations with the system. His orientations, thus, still tend to be negative, but his awareness of the system tend to make him at least potentially a factor that has to be considered carefully in any given situation.

The *subject political culture* occurs where there is a high frequency of orientations to the system as a whole and to its specifically output aspects. On the other hand, orientations towards the input objects and towards the self as political actor are absent. The subject's positive orientations may manifest themselves as pride in or hostility towards the system in general and its output aspects in particular. To both of these he may or may not accord legitimacy.

The subject's position, however, is essentially a passive one. He sees no possibility of influencing the system as it stands, and acquiesces by accepting as authoritative and unchallengeable the decisions of office holders. He interprets his role as one in which he must accept the system as it is, not try to change it, and obediently follow the instructions of his political leaders. Society is seen as possessing an essentially hierarchical structure in which all individuals and groups have a well-defined place with which they ought to be content.

In a *participant political culture* new attitudes emerge in society at large. The individual is seen, and sees himself, as an active member of the polity. He has rights and duties which he is expected to be consciously aware of, and where necessary, to exercise. The participant is oriented to all four types of political object—to the system in general, to its input and output aspects, and to the self as a political actor—and his knowledge of these objects is matched by a sense of involvement with and consciously made judgments on them. Evaluation and criticism of the system exists at all levels, and it is generally accepted as desirable that political activity should be under the close scrutiny of individuals and groups within society.

The orientations of the participant can involve favourable or unfavourable responses to the various types of political object. Correspondingly his feelings and evaluations of his role(s) vary from ready acceptance to open rejection of the system.

None of these models of political orientation, by itself, presents, nor was it intended that it should present, an accurate picture of the cultural environment of any empirical political system. Political cultures are never completely homogeneous; individuals in any given political system are not uniformly oriented to political action. For example, with a predominantly participant political culture there will be individuals who are not consciously aware of the existence and authority of central government agencies, and others who limit their political activities to obeying duly constituted law, which they may regard as expressions of national aspiration in which they take great pride.

To use Almond's classification to describe a political culture therefore indicates only the *predominant* patterns of orientation to political action within a given society. It does not imply that all individuals are oriented in the same way or to the same extent. Thus within a participant culture there may (invariably will) exist many individuals who are oriented only as subjects and/or parochials.

This means that Almond's three types of political culture are not seen as existing on a continuum in which one develops from another as structural patterns become more and more complex. The parochial individual does not become a subject by giving up one set of orientations when he develops another and participants are not produced by individuals relinquishing their subject and parochial orientations. Instead they develop an additional set of orientations '. . . that may be added to and combined with the subject and parochial cultures'.[4]

No political culture exists in the pure form which Almond's three models portray, and, to convey more accurately the nature of those political cultures in which there are significant proportions of more than one pattern of orientations he develops the notion of systemically mixed political cultures. These are (1) the parochial-subject culture, (2) the subject-participant culture, (3) the parochial-participant culture, and, (4) the civic culture, which combines all characteristics of all three 'pure' types of political culture.

The student of politics, however, cannot content himself with identifying cultural and structural patterns of the momentary situation. Political systems are only meaningfully understood when viewed over a period of time. Political cultures and structures are never stationary and it is the relationship between the two through time that provides the key to understanding political development and the distinguishing characteristics of particular political systems. This can be measured in terms of the congruence between political culture and structure.

Congruence is said to exist when popular cognition of the system tends to be accurate, and where the resulting sense of involvement with and judgments on the system tend to be favourable. In periods of rapid cultural and technological change many political systems are not in a state of congruence, and can best be depicted as moving away from and/or towards congruence. Many systems are best described as being in a perpetual state of incongruence. There is no inevitable tendency for a movement towards or away from congruence to complete itself. It is possible for cultural patterns to stabilize at a point short of congruence, that is, where individuals have accurate knowledge of the political system which they are prepared to tolerate but with which they have no sense of involvement or about which they have no positive, favourable opinions. Alternatively, a pattern of development may be established in which slow cultural changes are accompanied by slow structural changes, thus maintaining a balance between the two which closely approximates, but never actually achieves congruence. This pattern of development is particularly likely to appear in those societies in which individuals are positively oriented to the input process, that is, in situations in which popular volition can make itself felt, or at least where popular opinions are politically influential when called into being by a rival set of leaders.

TYPES OF POLITICAL SYSTEM

Almond uses these concepts of structure and culture to outline four distinct types of political system to be found in the contemporary world. They are (1) the Anglo-American systems, (2) the Continental European ones, (3) pre-industrial or partially industrial political systems and (4) totalitarian systems.[5]

The Anglo-American political systems are characterized by multi-valued political cultures, in which a large majority of the populace is firmly committed to the realization of some combination of the values of individual freedom, mass welfare, and security. At any one time there may be groups which stress one value at the expense of the others, but, in general, it is unlikely that any one of them will be completely repressed.

This culture is homogeneous to the extent that there is general agreement about political ends and the means to their realization. Politics takes on the atmosphere of a game; the result of the political struggle is constantly in doubt, and the rival groups of political leaders do not propose such radically different policies as to make the stakes so high as to convert the atmosphere of the game into that of the battlefield.

The political system is reminiscent of the market place; each actor has a well defined role, and a great deal of bargaining takes place between the various role incumbents. Policies are offered for sale in exchange for votes, and the outcome of the game (the power to decide) depends on gaining more votes than any of the competing groups of leaders.

Roles in Anglo-American systems are highly differentiated. Each party, pressure group, and voluntary association, has a specialized purpose or purposes, and performs a specialized function in the system as a whole. Each unit in the political system is manifest and bureaucratized, and almost all potential 'interests' in society play a part in the system and make their influence felt in the political process.

In addition to the complex and highly differentiated role structure, a striking feature of these systems is the stability of this differentiation. Not only do parliaments function as parliaments, bureaucracies as bureaucracies, and armies as armies, but it is inconceivable, for most of the time, that they could function as anything other than parliaments, bureaucracies, and armies respectively.

Lastly, the Anglo-American type of political system operates on the basis of a diffusion of power and influence. This is usually expressed in the ideological norms of the society, and reflected in the formal legal institutions of government. These are, of necessity, supplemented by real checks on power resulting from such developments as mass communication, mass education, and guarantees for all interests and groups to organize, be represented, and present the best possible case for themselves.

Continental European political systems—Almond refers mainly to France, Germany, and Italy, and points out that the Scandinavian and Low Countries fall somewhere between the Anglo-American systems and the Continental ones—provide, in contrast, a very different picture from those of the Anglo-

American world. The political culture is fragmented rather than homogeneous: different sections of society have established different patterns of cultural development, and some are more developed than others. Consequently, instead of talking about the political culture, it is more meaningful to speak of a series of political subcultures. These are caused, not by the introduction of such foreign cultural elements as are found in countries that have a history of subjection to imperialist and colonial rule, but by some sections of society developing cultural patterns in accordance with industrial and technological innovations while others have not.

In each of these systems there survives a pre-industrial subculture associated with the Roman Catholic Church, and established in those areas that are the least industrialized and secularized. A second type of subculture is that of the modernized, industrialized, parts of society. These sections of society aspire to a participant political culture, in which all individuals and groups are positively oriented to all political objects, and political life assumes the atmosphere of the 'market place'. These aspirations are thwarted however, because the other subcultures are only partially oriented to industrialization, and only partially secularized, and tend to be unaffected by the norms of the participant culture.

The cultural patterns of these Continental systems are complicated even further by the fact that since the nineteenth century, political issues have involved the very existence of these subcultures—anti-clericism, for example, which has existed in these societies since the first half of the nineteenth century in an attempt to reshape the orientations of those committed to a pre-industrial political culture. In addition, each subculture tends to be divided within itself. Each has elements which are more intransigent in their attitude towards other sections of society than are the rest. Thus, the middle-class subculture has one wing which draws towards the clerical, pre-republican attitudes of the pre-industrial culture, and another wing which is more inclined towards the anti-clerics and socialists of the industrialized sector of society.

The bargaining and compromising which characterized the Anglo-American systems is absent here. Each cultural subsection of society has conflicting and mutually exclusive designs for the political culture and the political system. Political affiliation becomes more an act of faith than a starting point for negotiation between competing political actors.

These Continental systems give rise to large numbers of militants, each convinced of the desirability and superiority of the norms of his particular subculture, and each prepared not to exchange, compromise and adapt to the viewpoints of others, but to preach, exhort, and, if necessary, stamp out all others in holy anger.

In these systems political roles are not attached to the system as a whole, but become embedded in the subcultures themselves. Each subculture develops a separate subsystem of roles, which means that the various subcultures become the focal points of the whole system. This is in contrast to the Anglo-American systems in which the formal legal role structure forms the key to understanding the interactions of the system. Consequently, in these Continental systems, there results a general lack of mobility between role incumbents in the various subsystems. Such intransigence means that at all times there exists within these systems a totalitarian potentiality. The rigid boundaries which separate the subcultures are always endangered by, and are sometimes swept by, movements of charismatic nationalism using coercive methods to transform a naturally fragmented political culture into a synthetically homogeneous one.

Like the Continental European systems, the pre-industrial or partially industrialized systems have a mixed political culture which contrasts with the homogeneous cultures of the Anglo-American systems.

Here, however, the cultural mix is very often the result of an imperialist or colonial era in the country's history in which a

Western type culture was introduced and superimposed on the traditional political culture or cultures. The precise nature of this mix depends on a number of factors which include for example, the type and character of the traditional culture(s), the agency through which the Western culture was introduced (by a Western colonial power or by a native elite), and the speed and methods by which Westernization was introduced.

The erosion of traditional political cultures often results in tensions appearing in society. Individuals and groups become concerned about the violations of customs and traditional relationships and accepted norms of behaviour; they develop a sense of insecurity, which often manifests itself in violent outbursts against the emergent system. Yet again the conflict of political cultures often results in the appearance of charismatic nationalism attempting to consolidate the new cultural norms, or to reaffirm those of the traditional cultures, or to establish a combination of the two. Charismatic nationalism provides a new course of legitimacy in the system, and as such, if it is to succeed, must be capable, if necessary, of overcoming traditional prejudices and of replacing previously established loyalties.

This type of system has a high potential for violence, which is caused by difficulties of communication and co-ordination which result from the fact that large groups within the system have radically different conceptions (cognitive maps) of the political system, and vastly different orientations towards its various aspects. Political interest tends to lie dormant for long periods, only showing itself in sporadic outbursts of spontaneous, violent action. Political parties tend to be unstable and ideologically incoherent; and bureaucracies, unless carried over from a period of Western colonial rule, tend to be only partially developed.

Unlike the Anglo-American systems there tends to be a high degree of role transference among political actors. Armies and bureaucracies often take over legislative functions; legislatures may interfere in judicial proceedings; and party decisions often pre-empt policy making functions. There is no stable division of labour.

Another characteristic of this type of system is that two or more political cultures may be operative within any one structure of roles. Thus, for example, within parliaments formally based on a set of legal norms and regulations which reflect the cultural orientations of Western type society there may operate powerful families, religious sects or tribal chieftains oriented to their own traditional culture patterns. Thus within such Western style institutions there are '. . . elements of the traditional role structure operating according to their own traditional norms'.[6] In describing the operation of these systems care must be taken to elucidate the nature of this cultural mix. According to Western norms many of the practices within these systems would be regarded as corrupt, but in the context of these culturally mixed systems they are perfectly acceptable 'normatively oriented' conduct.

In totalitarian political systems no voluntary associations are allowed to exist, communications are controlled by the agencies of government, and coercive force is monopolized by a rational bureaucracy controlled by a monolithic party. Due to these factors the political culture thus '. . . gives the appearance of being homogeneous, but the homogeneity is synthetic'.[7]

Most political systems are based on some concept of legitimacy, which acts as a unifying force in society. The authority of office holders is accepted by the individual because their positions have been gained by procedures which are generally accepted by society. In totalitarian systems, however, this 'acceptability' is artificially created. 'The characteristic orientation to authority tends to be some combination of conformity and apathy',[8] produced by the central control of the means of communication, and of the agencies of violence.

In such conditions coercive roles predominate. All organizations are surrounded by a coercive atmosphere; a characteristic which is buttressed by the unpredictability of the use made by coercion. All activity is subject to criticism by the state, and any activity can be arbitrarily defined as subversive or disloyal. Consequently, however great or however little the actual use of force in these systems, its impact is always present.

The lack of any stable delegation of power within the system prevents a diffusion of power and the establishment of centres of power other than the party. This leads to a general 'functional instability of power roles'.[9] The functions of the bureaucracy, army and secret police are expanded and contracted, introduced and abolished to suit the needs of the party. As circumstances change so these institutions are manipulated accordingly.

PART FOUR

Power

CHAPTER XII

Introduction

Power is a focal concept in political analysis, although surprisingly little consideration has been given to it in any depth until comparatively recently. Instead, the predominant orientation of a great deal of the history of Western political thought has been a concentration on the structures and institutions of political life. Relatively little has been said about the dynamic forces which operate within the political system; although, beginning with the works of Machiavelli, increasing attention has been paid to human factors in politics. From this perspective institutional arrangements and social structures are then identified as the mechanisms through which the drives and motivations of men can be satisfied.

In recent decades considerable interest has been shown in questions about what those who participate in politics hope to achieve from their endeavours. For those who adopt this perspective two immediate problems emerge: first, to identify what it is men strive for; and second, to establish appropriate methods for finding out who succeeds and who fails to get the most of what there is to have, and why. Thomas Hobbes, trying to answer the former question, suggested that man perpetually seeks power upon power as a means of maximizing the peace and security which he desires above all things. The two authors considered in this section have broadened their views of human motivations beyond this narrow desire for security postulated by Hobbes and have tried to identify the other values which man in contemporary society is concerned to 'possess'. Power, in their view, becomes merely one of a number of values which men seek, and in many instances it is sought only as an instrument for realizing some other more valued good.

The second question, that is how to study power empirically, is more problematical for the political scientist. Among the minor difficulties he has to deal with, is, on the one hand, the inherent limitations associated with direct observation of social processes: for example, the observer's inability to comprehend the totality of interactions, due sometimes to the sheer complexity of the situation, and sometimes due to the observer's own predilections and preferences. On the other hand there are the difficulties of publishing one's findings in such a way as not to offend the laws of libel and slander, or to transgress official secrets acts, or to lose the goodwill and co-operation of the personnel involved.

More important difficulties arise when questions are asked about how to identify the subject-matter of an inquiry into the locus and distribution of political power and influence. There is first of all the vexed question of 'what constitutes power'. Discussions of political power in the past have varied a great deal, stressing now one aspect of the concept, now another. They invariably show, however, that power is closely related to, and often confused with, other words and concepts, such as status, prestige, honour, deference, respect, and dignity. In specific situations each of these may provide some indication of a man's power, but in themselves do not constitute political power, and cannot alone provide a complete account of that power.

In order to understand the nature of political relationships and the characteristics of the power held by individuals and groups in specific situations it is essential that information be gained about the extent to which roles are differentiated, and whether authority and legitimacy are accorded an actor because of his own particular qualities or because of the roles he fulfils, or because of his social and economic circumstances. At its lowest level one must know whether, for example, an individual has power to influence *qua* individual or *qua* office holder. That is, knowledge of the source of influence and authority intimates a great deal about the society under consideration.

Discussions of power by political scientists in recent decades[1] reveal that there is still no agreed definition amongst them; there is neither uniformity nor precision in the use that is made of the concept. Even so, there are certain consistently developed, related themes which are relevant to different aspects of the study of politics. For example, relationships of power can be depicted in terms of command and obedience—a person (x) has power in so far as he can induce another (y) to act in a specific manner *because* he (x) has willed it. This general notion of power, however, relates in different ways to many different sorts of relationships in the real world, and by itself is, therefore, inadequate as a basis for a thoroughgoing *political* analysis. There is need to differentiate between the different sorts of influence in society in order to distinguish more precisely between the different kinds of relationships which persist between different actors. Perhaps the most obvious kind of power ('the production of intended effects' [2]) is exercised through the use, or threatened use, of physical force or some other kind of deprivation for non-compliance. This, however, does not exhaust the situations in which power relations exist, and indeed force alone would be insufficient to sustain a political system over a period of time. The commands of a human superior, if they are to be binding in the long run, must be accorded a degree of authority and legitimacy by those to whom they are addressed. Thus authority patterns and the norms which surround them constitute another set of power relationships which are of interest to the political scientist. Furthermore, it must be recognized that power is never exercised unilaterally and the actions of individuals and groups are too often made without adequate knowledge of all the factors involved for their decisions to act to be described as fully rational. Relationships of power are invariably of a reciprocal nature, such that if A controls B then B (to some extent at least) also controls A, and much of political life can be portrayed as a series of manipulative relationships pursued by the opposing forces in society who are competing for things that are valued.

The authors considered in this section each present a conceptual framework for studying power in society which takes into account such factors as these. Harold Lasswell concentrates his attention on identifying the things that are valued in society, and develops what he calls 'configurative analysis' as a means of showing the nature of changes in social values. Robert Dahl, on the other hand, attempts a classification of the processes of calculation and control which facilitate political activity and provide a basis for the relationships of influence and power in society.

CHAPTER XIII

Robert A. Dahl's Analysis

The student of politics must be interested not only in the differences between political systems but in their points of similarity too. The latter will help to define the subject-matter of his discipline, and also to place in proper perspective specialized studies within the broad field of politics. Dahl lists some of these common characteristics in his *Modern Political Analysis*. For example, competition for political leadership takes place, to a greater or lesser extent, among groups and individuals in all complex modern societies. This competition arises from, and results in, conflicts of aims, ideals and expectations among these various groups, and, in certain circumstances, the political system is the vehicle by which these sources of conflict are resolved.

Another common characteristic is that political influence is never evenly distributed throughout the populace. Some people are invariably more capable of influencing the behaviour of others than are their fellow citizens, that is, they have more control over political resources. For example, the division of labour, which is an inevitable attribute of contemporary society, means that some people gain greater access to the sources of power, prestige and wealth than others. This, in turn, gives them knowledge, experience and outlooks which are advantageous to them in the competitive struggles of political life. The combination of different social inheritances and innate differences of ability 'produce differences in the incentives and goals of different people in society'.[1]

A third point of similarity arises from the concern of all political leaders that their activities shall be willingly accepted as binding and authoritative; that people obey, not because they fear sanctions, but because they feel a sense of moral obligation, and that it is right and proper to heed leaders' decisions. This sense of legitimacy is encouraged through the development and espousal of a body of more or less coherent doctrine that seeks to justify and explain both the particular leadership and the whole political arrangements of society.

For the purpose of distinguishing between political systems, however, their differences tend to be more significant than their similarities. The criteria for differentiating are many and various, and must be selected for the purposes at hand and the aspects of politics in which one is interested. 'Just as there is no one best way of classifying people, so no single way of distinguishing and classifying political systems is superior to all others for all purposes.'[2]

In the history of political thought many classificatory schemes have been produced. Aristotle's famous schema, for example, distinguishes on the basis of the two criteria of the number of persons who share in ruling, and of the goals pursued by those in power. Weber, on the other hand, provides a basis for the classification of political systems according to the nature of the authority of the rulers. Such schemes inevitably simplify and distort. The realities which they are intended to categorize are rarely distinguishable solely in terms of a single or, at best, very limited number of criteria. The 'models' of the theorist are simple conceptual devices which facilitate the comparison and measurement of empirical approximations. This is done by showing how political systems deviate from these constructs of the theorist. The models, then, isolate the factors on which the comparison is to be made. If his work is to be useful, the theorist must avoid constructing models which are too vague to be operationalized, and must choose significant bases for making comparisons. The theorist, therefore, must attempt to produce models that are not too simplistic to prevent meaningful comparisons being made, nor so complex that they are not operationally viable.

Dahl, attempting this in his *Modern Political Analysis*, presents
a classificatory scheme by combining the criteria of Aristotle
and Weber with the further yardstick of the 'autonomy of subsystems' within society. Thus political systems are classified
according to (*a*) the number of persons who influence government decisions, (*b*) the type of authority on which the government is based, and (*c*) the independence and multiplicity of
sub-systems within the total political system. Using this scheme
systems can be categorized in sixteen different ways, and each
category presents a great deal of information about a system and
implies much more which can be tested and measured empirically. Such a scheme provides a framework which can orient the
empirical activities of the systematic student of politics.

Elsewhere, Dahl[3] presents another schema for studying political systems. He identifies four basic socio-political processes to
be found in all social systems and implies that actual systems can
be classified according to the variations of the relations between
these processes. The work transcends a discussion of political
systems in the narrow sense and attempts to incorporate both
economic and political theory to their mutual advantage. The
principal purpose of this study is to provide 'a political economy
of welfare "incorporating" certain aspects of politics and econo-
imics into a single body of consistent theory'. Its premise is that
analyses of social life, as well as attempts to achieve rational
social action, based on 'mythical grant alternatives' are doomed
to failure. The great issues (the isms) around which popular,
polemical discussions of political problems are often conducted,
provide inadequate bases for making meaningful social choices.
Socialism and capitalism, planning and laisser-faire, regulation
and the free market are not suitable conceptual tools for understanding and explaining the social systems of the modern world.
In Dahl's view both rational social action (by political and
other leaders) and an understanding of socio-political systems
(by political and social scientists) are achieved by substantially
the same methods: that is, by 'painstaking attention to technical
details',[4] and 'the countless particular social techniques out of

which "systems" are compounded',[5] rather than through the intimations and intuitive logic of some 'universally valid' social philosophy.

Many of the difficulties involved in the concept of rational action are avoided by Dahl who postulates simply that 'social action is rational or irrational depending on whether it achieves the ultimate ends towards which it is directed'.[6] Thus the criterion for rational action is simply the attainment of ends. Unlike Max Weber's concept of rational action it is unnecessary for the actor to be systematically and consciously oriented for his activity to be rational in Dahl's terms. Nor is it necessary that he should perceive correctly either the situation within which he acts, or the significance of his part in that situation. Dahl freely accepts 'the essential rationality of much unconscious behaviour'.[7]

Any concrete study hoping to use this scheme must initially deal with two outstanding problems: first, the goals, in terms of which the rationality or irrationality of social action will be measured, have to be specified, and secondly, the constituent processes which make up rational social action have to be identified. In the course of discussing these Dahl presents the outlines of a scheme for assessing the distribution of values in society and for identifying the nature of political relationships in various situations.

There are numerous ways in which the former problem can be approached. One could be purely empirical, taking as goals those values or aims about which there is some consensus in society; or one could derive a scheme of 'ends' from the utterances of selected leaders, party manifestos, the press, or ideological treatises. Alternatively, one could adopt the methods of Dahl and postulate, more or less intuitively, a system of goals which are to be used as yardsticks for assessing the various socio-political processes as means of achieving rational social action. He nominates seven basic goals toward which social action is directed, and the extent to which they are realized determines the rationality of the socio-economic processes adopted by society.

They are the goals of freedom, rationality, democracy, subjec-tive-equality, security, progress and appropriate inclusion. These are not, of course, the only goals towards which social actions are directed. Others include respect, self-respect, power, skill, love, affection, enlightenment.[8] Which goals one selects for assessing political systems is, to some extent, a matter of prefer-ence, and is largely determined by one's own purposes and the degree of specificity that one's inquiries can attain. Dahl explains his choice of goals, for example, on the grounds that they 'govern both the degree to which these prime goals of individuals are attained and the manner of deciding who is to attain his goals when individuals conflict in their goal-seeking'.[9]

Now the second problem must be examined. Rational action can only be sustained through time if individuals and groups make rational calculations about the best means of maximizing their goals, and if they are able to control, where necessary, the responses of others in the process of goal attainment. Rational calculation in many areas of social life is hampered by, for example, a lack of, and difficulty in acquiring, information about problems. Thus competent decisions are often prevented from emerging, or emerge only by accident. Furthermore, in the contemporary world many problems involve a large number of complex, interrelated variables which it is quite impossible for the individual to understand without assistance. Man's ability to overcome these problems is curtailed by such factors as his limited capacity for sustained rational thought, and the extent of his knowledge in any given field at any given time. Even so, there are certain techniques that have been developed which can help to minimize these difficulties. For example, infor-mation is best communicated if it is first codified so that the vast array of unsystematized data is presented in an orderly, consist-ent and simplified form. Decisions are then more likely to be rational if they are preceded by discussion of the codified mater-ial. Other techniques for reducing the complexities of modern social life to more manageable proportions for the analyst have also been developed. For example, sampling techniques enable data to be gathered and meaningful generalizations to be made about complicated social phenomena. These, in themselves, facilitate an understanding of such phenomena, and thus are conducive to rational calculation as a precursor of making decisions. Or again, social actions can be organized so that various functions are delegated to specialists or representatives, with the result that deciding is made much easier because each individual or group is concerned only with a limited number of variables apropos any particular decision.

Completely rational action can never be fully achieved because of the residual problem of man's innate limitations and the constantly changing complexities of the society about which decisions have to be made. However, by the use of the techniques available, and by a judicial use of such selection procedures as voting and market choice, the problems which confront society can be dealt with meaningfully. Dealing with social problems, however, is not simply a matter of providing means of calculating rationally what the alternatives in any given situation are. Processes of control must also be instituted if rational decisions are to be meaningful. These are not, of course, always different processes. Some, like the electoral process and the market mechanism, are processes which facilitate both rational calculation and control.

Control within a political system is exercised through a relation or set of relations among the actors. It exists when one actor induces other actors to act in some way they would not otherwise act. The degree of control varies from situation to situation and is often dependent upon the relative resources and methods of the actors involved. Dahl distinguishes four basic techniques of control, which can be discerned not only in political relationships but more generally in economic and social life as well.

First, there is control which is exercised unintentionally, as when investors are induced to buy shares as a result of a favourable market report designed only to provide information. This is called *spontaneous field control*: the activities of one actor uninten-

tionally produce new perceptions in others, and these perceptions, in turn, lead them to react in a particular way.

The second type is *manipulated field control*. This very often
develops from the first kind of control; for example, when people
learn over a period of time that certain actions invariably produce particular responses in others. Initially the actions may
have been performed for purposes quite unconnected with the
response, but once the connection between the action and the
reaction are realized, a person can, for a time at least, secure
definite responses from others in certain limited situations. Good
examples of this type of control are numerous in the political
sphere, as when politicians, with knowledge and experience of
the responses of an electorate, make innuendos against their
rivals or promise 'appealing' policies during election campaigns
in the expectation that public reaction will be to their advantage rather than to that of their competitors.

A third type of control takes the form of the issuing of *commands*. One controls by command when the responses of a subordinate are determined exclusively by the threat of deprivations
and sanctions being imposed as a result of non-compliance with
the stipulated directive. Politically this form of control is of marginal importance. Among the motives people have for responding to given situations fear of punishment does not rank very
high. Even the law is obeyed, in the main, because of the internalized norms of the subject rather than because of his fear of
being punished. If people are not disposed to obey, the law has
little power to control their behaviour. An example of its failure
to do so was the abortive attempt to enforce prohibition in the
U.S.A. in the 1920's. Control through command, therefore, is of
marginal importance in ordering human activities, and must, to
be effective over a period of time, be supplemented by other
techniques of control also.

These three forms of control have been represented as simple
unilateral relationships. That is, control being of one person or
group by another. In practice, however, social relationships are
usually far more complicated. When A controls B he (A) is also

controlled, to some extent at least, by B. Moreover, the actions of any one actor are rarely determined solely by any one other actor: one's activities are responses to the total situation in which one finds oneself; relationships are often neither unilateral nor bilateral but multilateral. Each actor is thus controlled by the combined influence of many other actors. Furthermore, the various kinds of control—spontaneous, manipulated, and command—are often super-imposed on each other, and thus complicate even further the problems of explaining actors' responses.

Out of this complex picture emerges Dahl's fourth technique of control—*reciprocity*. This exists when two or more people control each other through the techniques of manipulation or command or both.

Societies cannot be distinguished on the grounds that some use one technique of control while others use different techniques because 'the elementary techniques of control are present in all complex economies'.[10] The differences between various societies therefore can best be appreciated in terms of their similarities, or more precisely, in terms of the different ways in which they combine the use of similar control techniques.

The basic social processes for calculation and control are the means of realizing the goals which society has adopted. They are also the material which the student of politics must assess in his attempt to determine how operationally efficient various social and political arrangements are. By themselves, however, mere descriptions of these basic processes tend to be of limited value as means of categorizing and understanding the operation of actual political systems. Consequently Dahl proceeds to construct models of 'four central socio-political processes' which incorporate and support the processes of calculation and control, and are sufficiently precise to form the basis for a typology of political systems. The four processes are distinguished by the nature of the relations which would exist under idealized conditions between leaders and non-leaders. They are respectively, *the price system* in which there is no central control, *hierarchy* in which 'leaders exercise a high degree of unilateral control over non-leaders',[11] *polyarchy* in which 'non-leaders exercise a high degree of control over governmental leaders',[12] and *bargaining* in which there is 'reciprocal control among leaders'.[13]

None of these relationships exists in 'pure' form because the influence of other social processes encroach on the operation of each of these models and thus modify the relations that would otherwise pertain. Nor is any of these relationships exclusive to any society or group of societies. All societies exhibit each of the four kinds of relationships, but in varying degrees. 'Some relationships predominate in totalitarian societies and others in constitutional democracies; but specific instances of certain kinds of relationship can be found in both.'

THE PRICE SYSTEM

The price system operates mainly in the economic sphere. Problems arising from a modern industrial economy are brought within manageable proportions by reducing the number of variables with which any one person has to deal when deciding on a course of action. This is accomplished by representing the values of a very large number of commodities in terms of a common denominator—price. The exchange value of every commodity is expressed in terms of price thus making each commodity strictly comparable with every other commodity. This simplifies enormously the problem of making rational choices regarding, for example, the buying and selling of resources, materials, consumer goods, or the choice of occupation.

Consequences of this type of arrangement are the disappearance of central authority, and the system becomes self-regulating because the price of each commodity is determined simply by the interaction of supply and demand for that commodity or its substitutes. The complexities of fulfilling the leadership function are reduced considerably by this system. Each leader, like every other actor, makes decisions by considering only a relatively small number of variables and alternatives. Under idealized conditions leaders do not function differently from non-leaders and are to be distinguished from the latter only by the size of their transactions and the share of the market which they command.

Control in the price system is of the reciprocal type. In production, for example, leaders (businessmen) are controlled by non-leaders (consumers) because the demands of the latter affect the quantity and quality of the goods supplied by the former. On the other hand, non-leaders are equally controlled by leaders because the elasticity of supply will affect costs which will, in turn, affect demands made by the consumer. And lastly, leaders are controlled by other leaders. Few commodities are unsubstitutable in a complex economy, and the supply of substitutes by competitors will affect the businessman's market, and hence will control his activities in the process of production.

The price system is a political system, in the sense that the power to make decisions lies with an elite of businessmen. They decide how much of each commodity will be produced, and what combination of the factors of production will be employed in doing so. This elite manipulates the economy but it does so in a responsive and responsible manner because the overall pattern of production is determined by consumer preferences. The consumers' purchases correspond functionally to the act of voting in the democratic state. Each purchase is a vote for the continuation of the policy of producing the commodity purchased. Thus under the price system the initiative for making policy lies in the hands of the decision-making elite rather than in those of the electors. Leaders' decisions are ultimately controlled by the reaction to their policies at the polls (i.e. the market), and by each leader's anticipation of electoral response (the elasticity of demand).

It is a system that operates primarily in the economic sphere, but its implications clearly extend to other areas of social life as well. For example, it affords the individual a degree of freedom to determine his own patterns of consumption, and to choose his occupation, and to deploy his resources according to his own volition. Given these characteristics and that they are peculiar to this type of system, knowledge of the extent to which the price system is used is clearly important for assessing the efficacy of social arrangements for realizing the goals postulated by Dahl, or any set of goals which includes freedom of the individual.

HIERARCHY

Hierarchy is the term used by Dahl to refer to what is more commonly known as bureaucracy. Elements of it are found in almost all organizations in an industrial society, and it is characterized by relationships of unilateral control. In practice, pure unilateral control is rarely found since all human beings tend to be affected, and thus controlled (albeit minimally) by the pressures, demands, and opinions of other human beings (*qua* human beings and *qua* role incumbents) with whom they interact. The title 'hierarchy' is, therefore, reserved for those organizations which exhibit to a 'very high degree'[14] the characteristics associated with hierarchy in pure conceptual form.

Two simple tests are suggested to distinguish, prima facie, hierarchical organizations from polyarchal and bargaining ones. First, there is no institutionalized procedure whereby non-leaders can peacefully displace leaders; and second, leaders usually decide who shall be consulted and when and how it shall be done.[15]

Hierarchical systems are distinguished by certain structural features. First, the institutional structure and the relationships of the personnel within the organization are adapted in order to realize most effectively the goals which have been prescribed by the top leaders who may exist inside or outside the formal organization. In practice, the institutional arrangements and the behaviour and attitudes of members of the organizations may not reach the ideal prescribed for rational calculation and control. However, to a greater extent than elsewhere, the arrangements, behaviour and attitudes in a hierarchical organization are governed by conscious efforts to adapt, as rationally as possible, means to ends. The conscious efforts may only be made by the top leaders and those who are responsible for arranging the organizational aspects of the enterprise. However, because of their superior position of control within the organization, their norms and values tend to be accepted by subordinates as a necessary prerequisite of personal success within the hierarchy.

Second, hierarchy is 'marked by a more or less lengthy chain of controllers and subordinates'.[16] Each individual (except, of course, those at either end of the 'chain') controls his subordinates and is in turn controlled by his superiors within the chain. Thus hierarchy assumes a 'pyramidal' structure. At the top there are relatively few people, and they can control the large number below them either *via* the chain of control, or, if they wish, more directly. The duties and functions, as well as the amount of discretion to be exercised by each actor are usually rigorously defined in a set of prescriptions emanating from the top leaders. As a result of these characteristics a high degree of specialization tends to occur in hierarchical organizations.

POLYARCHY

In the contemporary world a particularly important goal to which all societies are committed is political equality. Recent history, however, might suggest that this is nowhere being realized, that there are powerful forces at work intensifying what some 'elitist' theorists have seen as an inevitable tendency towards inequality of control. Manifestations of this tendency are the increasing power of executives throughout the world, the emergence of dictatorships in many countries in a short period of time, and the extensive use of propaganda techniques and mechanisms of force and coercion to ensure compliance with established authority over large areas of the globe. In the light of such evidence some theorists have claimed that an 'Iron Law of Oligarchy' operates in all societies, and is reflected in the entrenchment of a minority in authoritative positions and the perpetuation of social and political inequalities.

Dahl sees polyarchy as a technique for counteracting and containing such oligarchic tendencies and as a means of approximating the general goal of a democratic society. Polyarchy

is the term he uses to refer to some of the political arrangements in those countries which we normally call democratic.
The word 'democracy' is used to refer to the total systems of
these countries; systems which invariably incorporate not only
polyarchal techniques but hierarchical and bargaining ones
also. That is, administration is usually conducted on a hierarchical basis, and legislation is enacted after a certain amount of
bargaining has taken place between the various political and
other leaders. Polyarchal arrangements exist primarily to order
relations between elected leaders and ordinary citizens, but in
addition polyarchal arrangements ensure the primacy of the
elected political leader in his dealings with non-elected bureaucrats.

Polyarchy ensures that 'non-leaders exercise a high degree of
control over governmental leaders'.[17] This control is made real
and the system becomes operationally viable to fulfil the purposes for which it was established only if certain institutional
arrangements obtain. For example, elections must take place
and be conducted in an atmosphere which is free from coercion,
in which an approximation to adult universal suffrage exists
and where almost equal weight is accorded to every vote cast. In
policy matters non-elected officials must be subject to direction
by elected leaders, who, in turn, are subordinate ultimately to
elected non-leaders. Such a system can only operate in circumstances in which a great deal of freedom is guaranteed. The
degree of freedom must, of course, be curtailed so as to be consistent with the organization of mass parties which in modern
conditions are an integral part of polyarchy. Nor is this general-
ization nullified by the existence of areas in which one party is
entrenched. In this situation, responsiveness is maintained by
the threat of 'potential' competitors who could be called into
existence if the present incumbents proved too intransigent or
unresponsive. Information must be made accessible to all through
channels that are not unilaterally controlled by the government,
and freedom to organize politically and to present alternative
policies and candidates to the electorate must be allowed.

Polyarchy, then, is facilitated through institutional arrangements in which individuals acquire the power to make decisions by competing more or less freely for the people's vote. The extent of the control by non-leaders (a distinguishing characteristic of polyarchy) is determined primarily by the degree of freedom which surrounds this competitive struggle. The greater the degree of freedom, the more responsive must leaders be to the demands and pressures of the electorate if they (the leaders) are to succeed in future elections.

BARGAINING

The fourth technique identified by Dahl is that of bargaining. This is a form of reciprocal control among leaders, and as such, relatively few people are involved. Bargaining takes place in all societies, but its specific form and significance varies from one society to another. It is greatly affected by the other techniques used in society. In countries with polyarchal institutions bargaining is a complementary technique and the culminating point of the decision making process. The amount of bargaining in such societies depends to a large extent on the range of agreement which exists on basic values and goals. The greater the area of agreement the less bargaining needs to take place; conversely, the narrower the basis of agreement the more likely is bargaining to become a feature of the polyarchy.

In general, bargaining is 'inversely related to the amount of hierarchy'[18] in society. Nevertheless even in hierarchy-bound totalitarian societies bargaining is not completely absent: it still takes place among the top leaders, who often have differing interests, views and values, although it may not be accorded the recognition it receives in democratic societies. While totalitarian societies are not organized on a pluralist basis, groups of leaders with different interests, values, perspectives and goals tend to emerge, and they compete and compromise (i.e. bargain) with each other during the process of deciding on a course of rational social action.

The principal actors in the bargaining process include political leaders at all levels of party, government, and bureaucratic organizations, leaders of organizations which exist for non-political purposes (e.g. leaders in T.U.'s, business and religious organizations, professional associations, etc.), leaders of pressure groups and interest groups, mass opinion leaders (publicists, editors, reporters, columnists, broadcasters, etc.), and individuals of special prestige or status. Bargaining between such people takes place at all levels of decision-making prior to policy choices being made. How successful the process is in reconciling differences and producing consensus depends not only on external factors such as the area of basic agreement among participants but also upon subjective factors such as the will of each actor to reach agreement.

None of these four socio-political processes exists in isolation in any society; each has its strength and weaknesses, and therefore each has to be combined with others to produce a viable system for choosing rationally how the community's resources shall be deployed. The functions which the various techniques are suited to fulfil are to a large extent determined by their very natures. For example, choice and allocation in the centralized process of polyarchy and hierarchy are made very difficult because of the difficulties of gaining adequate cost information and, more specifically, of calculating the marginal costs of the factors involved. Their usefulness in the process of deciding is further curtailed because of the difficulties involved in gaining information about consumer preferences.

Similarly, the nature of the decentralized price system makes it completely unsuitable for certain purposes, and cumbersome for others. For example, a decentralized system of national defence in which each individual calculated the marginal costs of safeguarding himself from external aggression is not only undesirable but unfeasible because of the prohibitive costs of materials and manpower. Also, in contemporary conditions, the spheres of education and social services, such as sanitation, road building and the maintenance of a police force, must be centrally controlled.

The price system is a viable system only if it can guarantee some degree of certainty to the various actors that they will reap adequate rewards for their efforts. Under certain circumstances, therefore, it may not be the most suitable mechanism for achieving goals which at other times it can achieve quite easily. The goals may not be fulfilled sufficiently quickly, or only at the expense of other undesired results, such as an adverse redistribution of income in the community, or adverse consequences on persons other than those directly concerned in the various transactions.

Thus all these techniques are used in economizing in every social system. The way in which they are combined is the means for comparing and contrasting, and this combination will depend on such things as the ideology, values and long-term interests of groups, as well as on the immediate objectives of contemporary leaders. Dahl and Lindblom have used this schema to inquire primarily into the politics and economics of the U.S.A. It provides, however, another alternative to the many schemes that have been produced in recent years to facilitate the systematic comparison of political and social systems; and by identifying socio-political processes distinguished by the relations between leaders and non-leaders it sheds light on the distribution of power and influence in society.

CHAPTER XIV

Harold D. Lasswell's Analysis

Lasswell shares with the other writers considered in this book the conviction that the study of politics cannot be confined to a few specific institutions. He holds a broad conception of what the discipline of political science involves. It is, in his view, 'the study of influence and the influential'.[1] Thus 'the subject-matter of political science is constituted by power as a process'.[2] Politics exists throughout the whole matrix of society and this must therefore constitute the sphere of interest of the political scientist.

Unlike the others, however, Lasswell is not content with merely providing the conceptual tools for describing and analysing the systemic relations between parts of the political system. In his first published work, for example, he writes: 'One aspect of the task of the systematic student of politics is to describe political behaviour in those social situations which recur with sufficient frequency to make prediction useful *as a preliminary to control.*' [3] This is a theme which he has developed consistently during the subsequent four decades of his literary life. He has gained an international reputation as one who has provided great insights and blazed many trails towards a methodology of the social sciences. It must be emphasized, however, that a complete understanding of Lasswell's work will only be achieved if it is appreciated that he is concerned to supplement the tasks of describing and analysing with those of predicting and prescribing. This he sees as the complete fulfilment of the role of the social and political scientist.

The task which Lasswell has set himself can be summed up as providing answers to his famous questions: 'Who Gets What, When, How?' [4] This leads him, in one aspect of his work, to move the focus of interest from concepts of social order, role fulfilment and the interactive processes of politics to a study of the men who actually fulfil the roles. He is concerned to find out what provides their motivations: what they are striving for; what they hope to get out of political activity. Although he is still interested in the structures of political and social order and acknowledges their importance, he sees them as the relatively permanent constructs which provide the parameters of political life. His main concern is to identify and understand the drives and energies of the actors within the system, and to find out what enables some to succeed whilst others fail.

VALUES

Lasswell's attempt to answer the 'what' of the question 'who gets what, when, how' centres on an analysis of the 'qualities' which are valued by men in society, and for which they strive in their political activities. All human endeavours (in the political sphere at least) are regarded by Lasswell as attempts to realize one or more of these qualities or values; and success in these endeavours bestows status, rank and prestige in the eyes of the rest of society. Knowledge of the distribution of these values throughout society and how they came to be so distributed will thus present the student of politics with many insights into the nature of the political system.

The first problem with this kind of approach is to identify which of a man's ascribed qualities are considered to be of value by society. Different societies and even different parts of any one society may evaluate various qualities and accomplishments in different ways. What is valued in any specific situation is an empirical question to be answered at the outset of any inquiry.

In his *Politics* [5] Lasswell lists the values of deference, income and safety, but in other works, for example, *The Democratic Character*,[6] he expands the list to the following eight terms: power, respect, affection, rectitude, well-being, wealth, skill and enlightenment. He stresses, however, that these are not intended to be definitive statements of what it is men seek in social and political life, but merely a typical selection of the values which men can (and do) seek in society. As social and environmental factors change over time so men's perspectives alter and this in turn affects the patterns of values which they seek. He stresses that the three values enumerated in the former work do not conflict with the eight listed in *The Democratic Character*: safety can be-equated with well-being; income with wealth; and deference to an amalgam of power, respect, affection and rectitude. Skill and enlightenment would thus appear to be of value as instruments for enhancing a man's realization of the other more basic values.

Elsewhere Lasswell divides the eight value categories into two groups which respectively emphasize deference and welfare. The former is comprised of power, respect, rectitude and affection, whilst the latter includes well-being, wealth, enlightenment and skill. An individual's success or failure in seeking any of these values is measured in terms of *indulgences* and *deprivations*. Thus the relative success or failure of an individual in this respect can be expressed according to an *Indulgence/Deprivation ratio*.

The concept of value developed here may thus be applied in analysing situations in which values are sought either as ends in themselves or merely as instrumental factors in realizing, what for an individual actor may be, a more important set of goals. Lasswell thus indicates that there are close connections between the various values that men seek in society. That is, almost every value is to some extent exchangeable in terms of other values; and possession of one value usually (even if minimally in certain cases) improves one's actual or potential for possession of other values. Power provides a good example of this. Competition for power ('participation in the making of decisions'[7]) is a characteristic of all political societies, yet it is rarely desired for its own

151

sake. Rather, it is thought of as an instrumental value or necessary prerequisite for realizing other values. Substantively
'possession' of power is a necessary pre-condition of effecting, for
example, a political programme designed to promote the values
associated with 'social justice'. At a more personal level, political power may be a necessary prerequisite to the acquisition of
the values of deference and respect which often result from success or popular political activity. Conversely, however, a certain
degree of respect, deference and success is necessary before any
substantial power or influence can be exercised. Thus a high
indulgence rating in terms of any one value is difficult to achieve
without substantial ratings of other values as well.

CONFIGURATIVE ANALYSIS
The study of values constitutes the core material for identifying
the objectives of political activity, and for partly explaining the
different combinations of co-operation, hostility, competition
and tensions which permeate political life. It answers the 'what'
of his question. To understand the 'when' and 'how' of his triad
it is necessary to expand the scope of the analysis and to inquire
more generally into the nature of political processes. To this end
Lasswell has developed a number of conceptual devices, which
he subsumes under the heading of *configurative analysis*. Two of
the basic concepts used in this approach are *equilibrium* and
development.

Equilibrium analysis involves identifying and describing the
complex interactions between the important factors within the
political process, which affect the distribution of values. Lasswell identifies some of the categories which are to form the basis
of this type of analysis, for example:

1. *Actions*—'Overt acts of conscious striving' such as fighting,
negotiating, boycotting, etc. affect the possession and distribution of values in society in fairly clear ways. As a direct result of
such activities individuals will often cease to strive for particular
values, be deprived of them, or voluntarily alter the objectives of
their involvement in social and political matters.

2. *Symbols*—Symbols are instrumental to the exercise of political power and influence. They include ideologies in the broad sense of that term as well as the great variety of identifying, value-laden concepts like 'nation', 'state', 'class, 'race', or 'church'. Part of any equilibrium analysis must be to identify which are the orienting symbols in any particular situation. It is the words and concepts used by participants to describe a given situation, or which form part of a political dialogue which give the description or the dialogue its unique characteristics. Symbols in this sense help to instil certain habits of social behaviour, and to foster certain stereotype images in the popular mind, and generally facilitate the social propaganda which is a functional necessity for a stable polity.

3. *Demands*—Although the symbols used in political life do not necessarily accurately reflect the phenomena or situations to which they refer, there is none the less a complex interaction between such symbols and the real world. The demands (such as demands for peace, security, welfare, abundance) that are made on the polity and society affect the conduct of political life, the values sought and the symbols used.

4. *Practices*—The corpus of interactive behaviour which comprises political life (the shaping and sharing of political power) is fashioned by a number of practices and structures which give form to the activity as a whole. These practices include the institutionalized ways by which elites are recruited and trained, how policies are made and administered, the institutional arrangements and constitutional provisions around which the polity is organized, as well as the less formal tactics and practices which elites use in the competitive struggles of political life.

In Lasswell's view it is the continual task of the social scientist to pursue knowledge along the lines outlined in this notion of equilibrium analysis. In the modern world this is an ever present and increasingly pressing need as contemporary societies are in a constant state of flux, continually changing at unprecedented rates.

Even so, equilibrium analysis, although a vital and important part of this approach, will not provide all the necessary data for the social scientist to fulfil the task assigned him by Lasswell. The information provided by this mode of analysis is, in itself, static and inconclusive, providing little more than a fleeting glimpse of the whole process of politics at any given point in time. Social and political systems, however, exist through time and must be analysed in a way that will show their development from one state of equilibrium to another. Equilibrium analysis facilitates an analysis of the interaction of forces at definite points in time only and not of the changes which take place over a period of time. Lasswell therefore supplements this kind of analysis with what he calls *developmental analysis* in an attempt to provide a historical orientation to his work. In his view developmental analysis provides a framework within which the substantive significance of the results of equilibrium analysis can be assessed.

A premise of Lasswell's developmental approach is a belief in the notion of historical uniformities, a belief that there exist certain social situations the broad patterns of which recur with sufficient frequency to allow study in a scientific manner. He does not subscribe, however, to the view that there is an absolute law of historical development which determines what sort of changes take place in society at different points of its development. He rejects all claims, such as the Marxian claims for their theory of historical materialism, which postulate some definitive end or inevitable goal as the culminating point of the historical process. Instead he tries to link equilibrium and developmental analysis through the concept of 'elite-symbol changes', by which he refers to the combined influence of changes in the structure of elites in society, the principles by which elites are recruited, and changes in the nature of orienting ideologies over a period of time. In this way he believes it is possible to identify current trends in the political system and thus this approach makes possible the control and influence over social and political development which he believes must figure prominently as the goals of the social scientist.

Lasswell's approach to the study of politics indicates clearly his belief in the relevance of a psychological perspective to the development of a science of politics. His analysis of various types of political leaders in terms of psychopathic traits (for example, political agitators are often the victims of some kind of insecurity in early childhood, or the hard working, meticulous administrator is likely to suffer from feelings of inferiority) is indicative of his belief that many political movements grow and develop because participants divert deeply embedded personal feelings into public channels.

This interest in the relationships between political processes and personality types is understandable in the light of Lasswell's more ambitious goals for political science. Not interested in mere description and diagnosis he sees the analysis of political relationships as valuable only in so far as it enhances his understanding of human motivations in politics, and to the extent that it provides a basis for social control, or what he calls 'the politics of prevention'. One of his fundamental beliefs is that all psychological aberrations within the individual are politically dangerous, and must be controlled if the excesses associated with fanaticism, dictatorships and tyranny are to be avoided.

The politics of prevention cannot be achieved through the formal, public channels of political life, such as public discussion, legislation, popular participation in politics or a realignment of institutional arrangements. In Lasswell's view it is the activities of the social scientist which provide the main hope for avoiding the dangers of extremism. The politics of prevention must be based on accurate knowledge of what causes the tensions within individuals and what allows them to find outlets for these tensions in public channels, often taking the form of violence, persecution and conflict. As a result of assigning the social scientist this unique role and because of his continual interest in policy oriented research Lasswell makes a distinction between what he calls a *contemplative standpoint* and a *manipulative* one. The former concentrates on describing social processes, identifying the interdependence of variables and their causal connections, and predicting their development. The latter concerns itself with selecting goals, and attempting the rational control of social processes on the basis of analyses of the alternative course of action and their environmental factors. Lasswell's view is that these are not necessarily alternative roles for the social scientist but complementary ones which together produce an understanding of social problems. For him political science is thus simply one of a number of policy sciences—'that which studies influence and power'.

CHAPTER XV

Conclusion

It has been our purpose in the last two sections to describe a few recent attempts to provide a classification of national political systems, through the use of conceptual models which to varying degrees may be said to reflect specific sets of variables within certain types of political systems existing in the second half of the twentieth century.

Classification is one of the fundamental bases on which concept formation rests, and without which empirical political science cannot get off the ground. Classification procedures are used to discover meaningful types that facilitate the ordering and explanation of phenomena which form the subject matter of any scientific inquiry. Classification consists of identifying two or more criteria so that any element, institution or phenomenon within one's delimited field of study satisfies at least one of these criteria. Types thus established are mutually exclusive, and comprise and exhaust *all* phenomena within the field of study—for example, the famous Aristotelian classification, based on the criterion of how many persons govern—that is, one, few or many. All governments can thus be classified into either monarchies, aristocracies or polities (or in their corrupt forms tyrannies, oligarchies and democracies respectively), each of which is exclusive of the others. In Aristotle's schema the logical necessity of numbers gives the types their exclusiveness of each other, and exhaustiveness of all phenomena—that is, who else can govern besides one, few or many? The same characteristics appertain to other classificatory schemes which stress the relative presence or absence of any given variable or set of variables:

for example, hereditary kingships versus republics, federal systems versus unitary states, developed versus under-developed polities, and so on. Logically all these pairs must be exclusive and exhaustive.

However, that a classificatory scheme satisfies certain logical requirements does not thereby guarantee its usefulness in promoting empirical inquiry. Classifications, to be useful, must reflect the various groupings of phenomena that are discernible in the real world. Criteria for such schema are many and various and must be decided upon in the light of one's immediate purposes as a political scientist, and of the nature of the material that one is dealing with. It would, for example, be possible to classify political systems according to the heights of ministers of finance or the obesity of heads of state—but it would hardly be a useful exercise and unlikely to result in an expansion of our knowledge of the relevant essentials concerning the structures and functioning of politics.

The problem is, therefore, to select meaningful and useful criteria on which to base a classification of phenomena. This partly explains the plethora of taxonomies that have appeared in recent years. Which criteria are meaningful and useful; which are likely to yield decisive insights into the nature of things political; or how one can best gain information about the particular aspect of politics in which one is interested—these are largely matters of subjective opinion, dependent upon one's particular purpose or purposes while making the analysis. The validity and usefulness of a classification is determined by its utility in the strategy of inquiry. In this sense, a fruitful classification (one with high explanatory power) will use classificatory criteria that are highly associated with and yet logically independent of other variables, characteristics and behaviours of the classified entities.

Thus Aristotle's criteria, or Weber's divisions on the basis of the characteristics of the authority held by rulers, were useful and illuminating as they were capable of describing many dis-

tinct political institutional arrangements, conducts and aspirations associated with different types of political system.

Similarly contemporary taxonomies emphasizing the distinctions between modern and developing systems, stable and
unstable democracies and dictatorships, Continental, Anglo-
American, pre-industrial and totalitarian systems will be useful
if, as is asserted by their authors, a large number of distinct and
exclusive traits, behaviours, structures, ideologies and political
styles can be associated with these categories. They may be used
as a basis for any attempt to explain and analyse the complexities of the many actual political systems that the political
scientist tries to make more intelligible.

It cannot be overemphasized that classificatory devices such
as those described in this section rely heavily on theoretical
insights, postulating, and not asserting, the association of the
various structures, behaviours and dispositions within the various types of political system. These 'models' imply systemic
relationships between the various aspects of the polity. They
are, however, abstract constructs claiming to go beyond simple
description by enunciating possible empirical laws about types
of political system. Whether, in fact, they will be borne out in
the real world, and whether their postulated types can be unam-
biguously identified among contemporary political systems can
only be determined by detailed analyses of those political
systems, using the types as the basis for the collection and col-
lation of data. It may be found that they are of limited utility and
validity in the empirical sense because their abstract, theoretical
concepts cannot be operationalized into observable categories.
Thus some typologies may prove to be inadequate because they
cannot be tested, whilst others may, when tested, prove to be
illusory.

Almond's classification of democracies into the Anglo-
American and the Continental European types provides a good
example of the kinds of difficulty which can arise when conceptual frameworks are measured against empirical reality.
Almond is most concerned to identify the degree of stability

within democratic polities, and his concentration on the cultural patterns of political life and the degree of role differentiation which exists complements the theses of scholars like Naumann, Duverger and Downs who argue that the institutional arrangements, in particular the number of parties, are directly related to both the quality and stability of the democratic polity. Quality is here taken to mean the ability of the system to establish and maintain 'the rights of the individual' and for governments to be both representative of and responsible to the electorate. A system's stability is seen in its ability to survive over a period of time, and to deal effectively with the internal and external pressures which confront it. The argument of these scholars is, broadly speaking, that a two-party system is inherently more stable and qualitatively superior to a multi-party democracy. The two-party system tends to be the more moderate because each party has to appeal to a broad cross section of the electorate and thus the extent of political divisions tends to be considerably reduced.

Almond's *Anglo-American* type corresponds very closely to these characteristics. Politics has the 'atmosphere of a game', and there is a homogeneous political culture which facilitates the autonomous existence of parties, pressure groups and the media of mass communication. Conversely the *Continental European* type systems are characterized by a fragmented culture and the mutual dependence of parties and groups. Implicit in this classification is the view that the former are inherently stable while the latter are inherently unstable.

These typologies of democratic systems—the Almond classification on the one hand, and the Neumann, Duverger, Downs perspective on the other—are based on a number of empirical generalizations about democracies, and provide a coherent and plausible set of theoretical propositions. More important than the internal logic and prima facie plausibility of these types, however, is the degree to which they can accommodate all democratic systems in the world, that is, the degree to which the typologies are exhaustive. To which category, for example, does one assign some of the smaller democratic systems of Continental Europe? Switzerland, Belgium, Holland and the Scandinavian countries are all stable democracies, yet each one operates on the basis of a multi-party system.

The theses of Neumann, Downs and Duverger based almost completely on the number of parties would appear to be illusory, or at least in need of substantial qualification. Sartori suggests[1] that not all multi-party systems are inherently unstable, and that a distinction needs to be drawn between 'moderate' and 'extreme' multi-party systems in which the essential dividing line falls between four-party and five-party systems.

Almond in his various writings appears to be well aware of the difficulties involved in his typology. He states specifically that the political systems of the Low Countries and Scandinavia 'stand somewhere in between the Continental pattern and the Anglo-American'.[2] Implicit here is a third type of democratic system whose details are never specified. To state, as the authors do, that these systems, while possessing many of the cultural characteristics of the two basic types of democracy, have developed 'their own version of a political culture and practice of accommodation and compromise' is to pinpoint the inadequacy of the typology as a whole, showing it to be incapable of exhaustively classifying extant democratic systems.

Clearly, at present the development of adequate empirical theories, on which fruitful classificatory schemes must be based, has not been taken very far. The first prerequisite for such developments must be the continued collection and analysis of cross-national data. Such work will indicate correlations and relationships among the variables of different political systems, thus indicating which are likely to be the most meaningful bases for comparison and contrast of political systems.

Notes and References

CHAPTER I

1 See, for example, D. Easton, *The Political System*; D. G. Hitchner and C. Levine, *Comparative Government and Politics*.

2 A recent analysis of the method of Marx in relating socio-economic conditions to political institutions is given by Raymond Aron in his *Main Currents in Sociological Thought*, Vol. 1: *Montesquieu-Comte-Marx-Tocqueville—The Sociologists and the Revolution of 1848*.

3 See the chapter on "The Emergence of Political Sociology" in W. G. Runciman, *Social Science and Political Theory*.

4 For some suggestions why Comte has not had a major influence, see the section devoted to him in R. Aron, op. cit.

5 W. Bagehot, *The English Constitution*, (1900), pp. vii–viii; Karl Marx, Preface to the first German edition of the first volume of *Kapital, Selected Works*, Vol. 1, p. 452.

6 Graham Wallas, *Human Nature in Politics*, pp. 38, 104.

7 Examples of this can be seen in many of the papers collected in H. Eulau, *et al.* (eds.), *Political Behaviour: A Reader in Theory and Research*.

8 Weber's analysis of authority is the focal point of much of his sociology of politics. He argues that ultimately all political authority rests on force, but the stability of a political system depends on this force being recognized as legitimate by members of society. He then constructs three 'ideal types' of authority which exemplify the ways in which this legitimization can take place. The three types are the 'traditional', the 'rational-legal' and the 'charismatic'. This typology is presented as being objective, inclusive and valid for all times and places. Weber insists that his types (or models) do not describe any actual system, nor do they offer a set of prescriptions for organizing political life. They are designed simply as 'heuristic tools', simply to provide a logical yardstick for studying authority, because every political system rests on some combination of

the three basic types. See Max Weber, *The Theory of Social and Economic Organization*, esp. Part 3; H. H. Gerth and C. Wright Mills (eds.), *From Max Weber*.

9 A useful discussion of 'ideal types' can be found in D. Martindale, "Sociological Theory and the Ideal Type", in L. Gross (ed.), *Symposium on Sociological Theory*. A rather critical discussion of some of Weber's ideas is given in S. Andreski, *Elements of Comparative Sociology*.

10 Parsons' writings are voluminous. As an introduction see T. Parsons, "An Outline of the Social System", in T. Parsons, *et al.* (eds.), *Theories of Society*.

11 A. F. Bentley, *The Process of Government*; D. B. Truman, *The Governmental Process*.

12 H. D. Lasswell, *Psychopathology and Politics*; H. D. Lasswell and A. Kaplan, *Power and Society: A Framework for Political Inquiry*; Charles Merriam, *Political Power*.

13 R. Dahl, *Modern Political Analysis*. See also for a recent overview, D. Cartwright, "Influence, Leadership, Control", in James G. March (ed.), *Handbook of Organizations*, pp. 1–47.

CHAPTER II

1 A useful discussion is to be found in Thomas P. Jenkin, *The Study of Political Theory*.

2 For some political analysis pursuing this approach, see A. Brecht, *Political Theory*; P. Laslett (ed.), *Philosophy, Politics and Society*; T. D. Weldon, *The Vocabulary of Politics*; and, in general, V. Van Dyke, *Political Science: A Philosophical Analysis*.

3 See as an example, J. G. March, "An Introduction to the Theory and Measurement of Influence", *American Political Science Review*, Vol. 49, 1955.

4 G. A. Almond, "Political Theory and Political Science", *American Political Science Review*, Vol. LX, 1966, pp. 869–79; R. A. Dahl, "The Behavioural Approach in Political Science: Epitaph for a Monument to a Successful Protest", ibid., Vol. LV, 1961, pp. 763–72.

5 For the traditional view, see M. Wight, "Why Is There No International Theory?", in H. Butterfield and M. Wight (eds.), *Diplomatic Investigations*.

6 D. Easton, *The Political System*, p. 65. As another author has recently remarked: 'raw data must still . . . be manipulated, re-arranged and combined in order to be theoretically useful'. D. Singer, *Quantitative International Politics: Insights and Evidence*.

7 Ibid., pp. 52-3.

8 Norwood Hanson, *The Concept of the Positron*, p. 44. Our italics.

9 An interesting discussion of these problems, though in the context of international relations, is given by a 'modernist', M. A. Kaplan in "The New Great Debate: Traditionalism vs. Science in International Relations", *World Politics*, Vol. xix, No. 1, 1966, pp. 1–20.

10 Peter Achinstein, "Theoretical Models", *British Journal for the Philosophy of Science*, Vol. 16, 1965, p. 105.

11 A discussion of these problems, especially useful because it relates to a particular problem of contemporary political analysis is that given by F. J. Fleron, Jr., "Soviet Area Studies and the Social Sciences: Some Methodological Problems in Communist Studies", *Soviet Studies*, Vol. xix, No. 3, 1968, pp. 314–39; on "Various Meanings of 'Theory' ", see Anatol Rappoport, *American Political Science Review*, Vol. lii, 1958, pp. 972–88.

12 G. A. Almond and J. Coleman (eds.), *The Politics of the Developing Areas*, pp. 3–4.

13 L. Bertallanfy, *Problems of Life*, pp. xi–xix.

14 Almond and Coleman, op. cit., p. vii.

15 D. Easton, *A Framework for Political Analysis*, pp. 24–5. See further the chapter in this book related to the work of Easton.

16 Dorothy Emmet, *Function, Purpose and Powers*, p. 293.

17 See Easton, op cit., p. 37.

18 G. A. Almond and S. Verba, *The Civic Culture*.

CHAPTER III

1 A. N. Prior, *Formal Logic*, p. 20.

2 J. Joos, *Theoretical Physics* (London: Blackie, 1951) p. 1, quoted in H. Hanson, *Patterns of Discovery*, p. lxx.

3 See the essays in D. Easton (ed.), *Varieties of Political Theory*.

CHAPTER IV

1 G. A. Almond and G. B. Powell, Jr., *Comparative Politics: A Developmental Approach*, p. 215.

2 Ibid., p. 171.

3 Ibid., pp. 207, 208.

4 From the Greek *telos*, meaning 'end'. For a discussion of teleology and its use in Aristotelian social theory, see D. Emmett, op. cit., pp 49–52.

5 e.g., 'The problem of developing categories to compare the

conversion processes in different kinds of political systems is not unlike the problem of comparative anatomy and physiology.'
G. A. Almond, "A Developmental Approach to Political Systems", *World Politics*, Vol. xvii, No. 2, 1965, p. 195.

6 Ibid., p. 188.

7 Most famous, perhaps, of modern works, is that by W. W. Rostow, *The Stages of Economic Growth*, though this has been subjected to extensive criticism.

8 G. A. Almond and J. Coleman (eds.), *The Politics of the Developing Areas*, pp. 16, 64. We shall in future refer to this as *The Politics*, and the work by Almond and Powell as *Comparative Politics*.

9 Almond and Coleman, *The Politics*, p. 7. Max Weber's definition of 'politics' and the 'state' or 'political association' from, as he puts it, 'the sociological point of view' can be found in H. H. Gerth and C. W. Mills (eds.), op. cit., p. 77 ff.

10 Almond and Powell, *Comparative Politics*, pp. 13–14. Almond, however, distinguishes his kind of 'systems analysis' from that of, for example, David Easton.

11 Talcott Parsons, *The Social System*; Marion Levy, *The Structure of Society*; see also Robert Merton, *Social Theory and Social Structure*.

12 T. Parsons, *The Social System*, pp. 297–8.

13 See *inter alia*, D. Easton, "Limits of the Equilibrium Model in Social Research", in H. Eulau, *et al.* (eds.), *Political Behaviour*, pp. 397–404.

14 Almond, "A Developmental Approach to Political Systems", *World Politics*, Vol. xvii, No. 2, 1965, p. 187. A useful critique of certain methodological shortcomings of functional analysis is that by R. E. Dowse, "A Functionalist's Logic", *World Politics*, Vol. xvii, No. 4, 1966, pp. 607–22.

15 Almond and Coleman, *The Politics*, p. 11.

16 Ibid., p. 17.

17 Almond and Powell, *Comparative Politics*, p. 25. In this work, Almond and Powell considerably expand the analysis of inputs and outputs introduced in *The Politics*. For this they use the recent work of David Easton.

18 This has been associated with the name of Leontief. See, for example, Wasily Leontief, "The Structure of Development", *Scientific American*, September 1963.

19 Almond and Powell, *Comparative Politics*, p. 23.

20 A discussion of this with respect to the work of Parsons can be found in D. Lockwood, "Some Remarks on 'The Social System' ", *British Journal of Sociology*, Vol. 7, 1956, pp. 134–46.

Models of Political Systems

21 Almond and Coleman, *The Politics*, p. 21.
22 Almond and Powell, *Comparative Politics*, pp. 255, 284.
23 Ibid., p. 94.
24 Almond, "A Developmental Approach to Political Systems", *World Politics*, op. cit., p. 191.
25 Almond and Powell, *Comparative Politics*, p. 191.
26 Ibid., p. 193.
27 Ibid., ch. xi. Almond's attempt at this approach.
28 Almond, "A Developmental Approach to Political Systems", *World Politics*, op. cit., p. 193.

CHAPTER V
1 Crawford Young, *Politics in the Congo: Decolonization and Independence*, p. 602.
2 Aristide Zolberg, "A View from the Congo", *World Politics*, Vol. XIX, 1966.
3 Stephen Toulmin, *The Philosophy of Science*, p. 34.
4 Easton, "Alternative Strategies in Theoretical Research", in D. Easton (ed.), *Varieties of Political Theory*, p. 5.
5 Easton, *A Systems Analysis of Political Life*, p. 488. We shall refer to this work as Systems Analysis.
6 Ibid., p. 8.
7 This form of analysis has been associated predominantly with the name of Harold Lasswell. See his *Politics: Who Gets What, When, How*.
8 Easton, *The Political System*, p. 134.
9 See, for example, the works of A. R. Radcliffe-Brown, *Structure and Function in Primitive Society* and *Andaman Islanders*, and also, B. Malinowski, *Argonauts of the Western Pacific*.
10 For the criticism of structural-functionalism see Easton, *A Framework for Political Analysis* (henceforth referred to as *A Framework*), pp. 105–6. The quotation is from Easton, *The Political System*, p. 279.
11 Easton, *The Political System*, p. 85.
   a. J. A. Schumpeter, "The Common Sense of Econometrics", *Econometrica*, I, 1933, p. 6.
   b. J. A. Schumpeter, *Business Cycles*, p. vi.
12 Easton, *The Political System*, p. 146. Easton's definition has, needless to say, been subjected to criticism. See, for example, among English critics, B. Crick, *In Defence of Politics*, pp. 177–8.
13 Easton, *Systems Analysis*, p. 15; also Easton, *A Framework*, p. 25. For doubt as to whether this should really constitute the focus of

inquiry, see B. Dudley, "Political Theory and Political Science", *The Nigerian Journal of Economic and Social Studies*, Vol. 7, No. 3, 1965, pp. 257–71.

14 A useful analysis of "The Concept of System in Political Science" will be found in an article with that title by J. P. Nettle in *Political Studies*, October 1966, pp. 303–38.

15 Easton, *A Framework*, p. 26.

16 Ibid., p. xiii.

17 Ibid., p. 77.

18 Ibid., p. 78.

19 Ibid., p. 88 and pp. 24–5.

20 Ibid., p. 88. Our italics.

21 Ibid., p. 82.

22 L. Bertallanfy, *Problems of Life*, p. 125. Author's italics.

23 Easton, *A Framework*, p. 112.

24 Ibid., pp. 74, 50.

25 Easton, *The Political System*, p. 132.

26 At this formal level, he does, as we shall see, allow (as other analysts do) that one of the components of a 'regime' is its system of values.

27 Easton, *A Framework*, p. 131.

28 Easton, *Systems Analysis*, pp. 57–69.

29 Ibid., pp. 153–70.

30 Ibid., p. 24. See also his discussion in *A Framework*, pp. 90–8.

31 Easton, *Systems Analysis*, p. 179.

32 For the definition of 'political community', see Easton, *Systems Analysis*, p. 177, and on this generally, pp. 171–89.

33 Ibid., pp. 192 ff.

34 Ibid., pp. 212 ff.

35 Easton, *A Framework*, p. 53.

36 See Leon Lindberg, "The Political Community as a Political System: Notes toward the Construction of a Model", *Journal of Common Market Studies*, Vol. 5, No. 4, 1967, pp. 344–87.

CHAPTER VI

1 David E. Apter, *The Politics of Modernization*, pp. 5–6.

2 D. Easton, *The Political System*, p. 319.

3 Apter, op. cit., p. x.

4 Ibid., pp. 10–11; for the previous quotation, p. 15; see also p. 229.

5 Ibid., pp. 229, 228.

6 Ibid., p. 431. Our italics.

7 David E. Apter, *Ghana in Transition*, p. v.
8 See Chapter 1.
9 David E. Apter, *The Political Kingdom in Uganda*, p. 3.
10 Apter, *The Politics of Modernization*, pp. 67, 157.
11 Ibid., p. 42.
12 It is this aspect of modernization that Fred W. Riggs has been concerned to emphasize in his studies of the 'ecology' of public administration. See, for example, F. W. Riggs, *Administration in Developing Countries: The Theory of Prismatic Society*.
13 Apter, *The Politics of Modernization*, p. xiii. Here, as in the work of Almond, there is a suggestion of teleological analysis, but one that does not specify a *particular* end—the process is 'open-ended'.
14 Ibid., p. 23. Our italics. See also pp. 732–4 of Apter's essay in D. Apter and H. Eckstein (eds.), *Comparative Politics*.
15 See ibid., pp. 231–5 for his discussion of Almond's approach and his discussion of 'the value of functional analysis' and of approaches which emphasize viability or survival. Almond's own approach was initially based on, in particular, Marion Levy's *The Structure of Society*.
16 Ibid., p. 25.
17 Ibid., p. 256, also p. 22 ff. for his discussion of the two models of government.
18 Ibid., p. 3. Our italics.
19 Ibid., p. 11.
20 Ibid., p. 40.
21 Ibid., p. 227.
22 On 'political religion', see ibid., p. 267 ff.; on ideology and the 'role of the ideologue', p. 313 ff. See also his discussion in D. Apter (ed.), *Ideology and Discontent*, pp. 16–17.
23 Apter, *The Politics of Modernization*, p. 397.
24 Ibid., p. 230.
25 Ibid., p. 231 ff. See also Apter, *Ghana in Transition*, for example, for his discussion of the functional requisites of chieftaincy and charismatic authority as types of government.
26 Apter, *The Politics of Modernization*, p. 172. Our italics.
27 Ibid., p. 75 ff. See in this connection, the discussion by Shils, below, Chapter VII.

CHAPTER VII
1 We are not here concerned with the chronological development of the thought of Deutsch and Easton. The major work of

Deutsch to which we shall make reference was published in 1963. See K. W. Deutsch, *The Nerves of Government*.

2 Deutsch, *The Nerves of Government*, p. 124. Our italics. See also p. 120. Parsons' view can be found in his "On the Concept of Influence", *Public Opinion Quarterly*, Vol. 24, 1963, pp. 37–62.

3 Ibid. The quotations are from pp. 124, 254. See also p. 222 for a definition of politics.

4 K. Deutsch, *Nationalism and Social Communications*, p. 75. Italics in the original.

5 Deutsch, *The Nerves of Government*, p. 151.

6 Ibid., p. 150.

7 Ibid., p. 122.

8 See Deutsch, "Communication Theory and Political Integration", in P. E. Jacob and J. V. Toscano (eds.), *The Integration of Political Communities*, p. 49.

9 Deutsch, *The Nerves of Government*, p. ix. See also p. 182.

10 Ibid., pp. 139–40.

11 Ibid., p. 129. On 'the classic concept of organism', see pp. 30–4.

12 Ibid., p. 79.

13 N. Weiner, *Cybernetics or Control and Communication in the Animal and the Machine*. See also W. Ross Ashby, *An Introduction to Cybernetics*.

14 D. Emmet, *Function, Purpose and Powers*, p. 61.

15 For descriptions of cybernetics analysis, see Stafford Beer, "The World, the Flesh and the Metal: The Prerogative of Systems", *Nature*, Vol. 205, 1965, pp. 223–31, who wishes to relate it to business management; and also, M. Caldwallader, "The Cybernetic Analysis of Change", in Amitai and Eva Etzioni (eds.), *Social Change*, pp. 159–64.

16 Deutsch, *The Nerves of Government*, p. 88.

17 Ibid., pp. 188–9.

18 Ibid., p. 185.

19 See his discussion of the 'probabilities of failure' of political systems, ibid., p. 223 ff.

20 Ibid., p. 246. See also p. 107.

21 Ibid., p. 50. See also his description of the 'indicators of political structure', in Jacob and Toscano (eds.), op. cit., p. 36. An attempt to use Deutsch's model for an international relations case study is made by Bruce Russett in his *Community and Contention: Britain and America in the Twentieth Century*. See especially Chapter 2, "The Basis of Political Community" for his discussion of concepts.

Models of Political Systems

CHAPTER VIII

1 S. Beer, "The World, the Flesh and the Metal", op. cit., p. 223.
2 Almond and Powell, *Comparative Politics: A Developmental Approach*, p. 192.
3 Karl Marx, "Preface to the First German Edition of the First Volume of Kapital", *Selected Works*, Vol. I, p. 449.
4 Especially in view of Easton's criticism of structural-functional analysis. See D. Easton, *A Framework for Political Analysis*, pp. 105–6.
5 K. Deutsch, *The Nerves of Government*, p. 80.
6 Ibid., p. vii.
7 D. Easton, *A Framework for Political Analysis*, p. xiii.
8 In the *Economic and Philosophical Manuscripts*. This translation is from T. B. Bottomore and M. Rubel, *Karl Marx: Selected Writings in Sociology and Philosophy*, p. 70. Italics in the original.

CHAPTER IX

1 See D. Apter and H. Eckstein (eds.), *Comparative Politics*, p. 4.
2 Ibid.

CHAPTER X

1 For an excellent discussion of the difficulties inherent in the terms 'developed' and 'developing', see W. J. M. Mackenzie, *Politics and Social Science*.
2 E. A. Shils, *Political Development in the New States*, p. 10.
3 Loc. cit., p. 10.
4 Shils, op. cit., p. 48.
5 Ibid., p. 51.
6 J. A. Schumpeter, *Capitalism, Socialism and Democracy*, pp. 294–5.
7 Shils, op. cit., p. 52–3.
8 Ibid., pp. 69.
9 Shils, op. cit., p. 81.
10 Ibid., p. 89.

CHAPTER XI

1 G. A. Almond, "Comparative Political Systems", *Journal of Politics*, Vol. 18, 1956, p. 396.
2 G. A. Almond and S. Verba, *The Civic Culture: Political Attitudes and Democracy in Five Nations*, p. 17.
3 See D. A. Rostow, "The Politics of the Near East", in Almond and Coleman (eds.), *The Politics of the Developing Areas*, pp. 378–9.

4 Almond and Verba, *The Civic Culture*, p. 20.
5 See "Comparative Political Systems", *Journal of Politics*, Vol. 18, 1956.
6 Ibid., p. 402.
7 Ibid., p. 403.
8 Ibid., p. 403.
9 Ibid., p. 405.

CHAPTER XII

1 See, e.g., Talcott Parsons, "Distribution of Power in American Society", *World Politics*, Vol. 10, October 1967; Robert Bierstadt, "The Problem of Authority" in *Freedom and Control in Modern Society* (eds.), M. Berger, T. Abel, and C. H. Page 1954; B. Russell, *Power: A New Social Analysis*, 1936.
2 Russell, op. cit.

CHAPTER XIII

1 R. A. Dahl, *Modern Political Analysis*, p. 15.
2 Ibid., p. 26.
3 R. A. Dahl and C. Lindblom, *Politics, Economics and Welfare*.
4 Ibid., p. 3.
5 Ibid., p. 6.
6 Ibid., p. 19.
7 Ibid., p. 25.
8 For a discussion and more complete list of individual goals, see the works of H. D. Lasswell, especially *Power and Personality* and *Politics: Who Gets What, When, How*.
9 Dahl and Lindblom, op. cit., p. 28.
10 Ibid., p. 93.
11 Ibid., p. 227.
12 Ibid., p. 227.
13 Ibid., p. 324.
14 Ibid., p. 227.
15 Defining who are leaders and who are non-leaders is, in itself, a complicated problem. Dahl suggests it can best be done by measuring the extent of the control exercised by each individual over other individuals. A useful discussion of this distinction between leaders and non-leaders is provided by H. D. Lasswell and A. Kaplan in *Power and Society: A Framework for Political Inquiry*. The extent of control is to be gauged by finding out how much influence an actor has over policy formation and over 'the persons whose policies are affected', and the scope of his

influence is to be determined by studying 'the values implicated in the policies'. Information of this kind will show who has 'significantly greater control' in an organization. These distinctions are not precise nor are they unambiguous, but in the absence of a more rigorous operational schema for distinguishing leaders, they are likely to yield the best possible results if used in a pragmatic and approximate way.

16 Dahl and Lindblom, op. cit., p. 235.

17 Ibid., p. 227.

18 Ibid., p. 324.

CHAPTER XIV

1 H. D. Lasswell, *Politics: Who Gets What, When, How*, reprinted in Lasswell, *Collected Works*, Free Press, Glencoe, Ill. 1951, p. 295.

2 H. D. Lasswell and A. Kaplan, *Power and Society*, p. xvii.

3 H. D. Lasswell, "Chicago's Old First Ward: A Case Study in Political Behavior", *National Municipal Review*, March 1923, p. 127.

4 This is the title of his work—*Politics: Who Gets What, When, How*, op. cit.

5 Ibid.

6 Lasswell, *The Democratic Character, Collected Works*, op. cit., pp. 465–525.

7 Ibid., p. 476

CHAPTER XV

1 Giovanni Sartori, "European Political Parties: The Case of Polarized Pluralism", in Joseph La Palombara and Myran Weiner (eds.), *Political Parties and Political Development*.

2 G. A. Almond, "Comparative Political Systems", *Journal of Politics*, Vol. 18, No. 3, August 1956.

Bibliography

This book has attempted no more than a brief introduction to the conceptual frameworks of some contemporary political scientists. It is hoped that the reader's interest will be stimulated not satisfied or killed. What follows are two lists of leading works dealing with the areas which we have discussed to which the reader eager for more may turn. The first cites the works which have been discussed at some length in this book; the second lists other, equally important, attempts at concept formation, as well as general discussions and critiques of contemporary approaches to the study of politics.

SELECT BIBLIOGRAPHY

Almond, G. A., "Comparative Political Systems", *Journal of Politics* Vol. 18, 1956,
——, "A Developmental Approach to Political Systems", *World Politics*, Vol. xvii, No. 2, 1965.
Almond, G. A. and Coleman, J. (eds.), *The Politics of the Developing Areas*, Princeton University Press, Princeton, New Jersey 1960.
Almond, G. A. and Powell, G. B., *Comparative Politics: A Developmental Approach*, Little, Brown & Co., Boston 1966.
Almond, G. A. and Verba, S., *The Civic Culture: Political Attitudes and Democracy in Five Nations*, Princeton University Press, Princeton, New Jersey 1963.
Apter, D. E., *The Politics of Modernization*, Chicago University Press, 1965.
Dahl, R. A. and Lindblom, C., *Politics, Economics and Welfare*, Harper, New York 1953.
Deutsch, K. W., *The Nerves of Government*, Free Press, Glencoe, Ill. 1963.
Easton, D., *The Political System*, Alfred A. Knopf, New York 1953.
——, *A Framework for Political Analysis*, Prentice Hall, New Jersey 1965.
——, *A Systems Analysis of Political Life*, John Wiley, London 1965.

Lasswell, H. D., *Politics: Who Gets What, When, How*, McGraw-Hill, New York 1936.

Parsons, T., "An Outline of the Social System", in T. Parsons *et al.* (eds.), *Theories of Society*, Free Press, Glencoe, Ill. 1961.

Shils, E. A., *Political Development in the New States*, Mouton and Co., The Hague 1960.

GENERAL BIBLIOGRAPHY

Achinstein, P., "Theoretical Models", *British Journal for the Philosophy of Science*, Vol. 16, 1965.

Almond, G. A., "Political Theory and Political Science", *American Political Science Review*, Vol. LX, 1966.

Andreski, S., *Elements of Comparative Sociology*, Weidenfeld and Nicolson, London 1964.

Apter, D. E., *Ghana in Transition*, Atheneum Press, New York 1963. First published in 1955 as *The Gold Coast in Transition*, Princeton University Press.

———, *Ideology and Discontent*, Free Press, Glencoe, Ill. 1964.

———, *The Political Kingdom in Uganda*, Princeton University Press, Princeton, New Jersey 1961.

Apter, D. E. and Eckstein, H. (eds.), *Comparative Politics*, Free Press, Glencoe, Ill. 1963.

Aron, R., *Main Currents in Sociological Thought*, 2 vols., Weidenfeld and Nicolson, London 1965; Basic Books, New York, Vol. I, 1965; Vol. II, 1967.

Ashby, W. R., *An Introduction to Cybernetics*, John Wiley New York, 1956.

Bagehot, W., *The English Constitution*, Oxford University Press, London 1928.

Beer, S., "The World, the Flesh and the Metal: The Prerogative of Systems", *Nature*, Vol. 205, 1965.

Bentley, A. F., *The Process of Government*, Indiana Press, Bloomington, Ind. 1949.

Bertallanfy, L., *Problems of Life*, Harper, New York 1952.

Bierstadt, R., "The Problem of Authority" in Berger, M., Abel, T., and Page, C. H. (eds.), *Freedom and Control in Modern Society*, Van Nostrand, New York 1954.

Bottomore, T. B. and Rubel, M., *Karl Marx: Selected Writings in Sociology and Social Philosophy*, Watts, London 1956.

Brecht, A., *Political Theory*, Princeton University Press, Princeton, New Jersey 1959.

Caldwallader, M., "The Cybernetic Analysis of Change", in

Amitai and Eva Etzioni (eds.), *Social Change*, Basic Books, New York 1964.

Crick, B., *In Defence of Politics*, Penguin, Harmondsworth 1964.

Dahl, R. A., *Modern Political Analysis*, Prentice Hall, New Jersey 1963.

——, "The Behavioural Approach in Political Science: Epitaph for a Monument to a Successful Protest", *American Political Science Review*, Vol. LV, 1961.

Deutsch, K., *Nationalism and Social Communications*, M.I.T. Press, New York 1953.

Dowse, R. E., "A Functionalist's Logic", *World Politics*, Vol. XVII, 1966.

Dudley, B., "Political Theory and Political Science", *The Nigerian Journal of Economic and Social Studies*, Vol. 7, 1965.

Easton, D., "Limits of the Equilibrium Model in Social Research", in Eulau, H. *et al.* (eds.), *Political Behaviour*, Free Press, Glencoe, Ill. 1956.

Easton, D. (ed.), *Varieties of Political Theory*, Prentice Hall, New Jersey 1966.

Emmet, D., *Function, Purpose and Powers*, Macmillan, London 1958.

Eulau, H. *et al.* (eds.), *Political Behaviour: A Reader in Theory and Research*, Free Press, Glencoe, Ill. 1959.

Fleron, F. J., "Soviet Area Studies and the Social Sciences: Some Methodological Problems in Communist Studies", *Soviet Studies*, Vol. XIX, 1968.

Gerth, H. H. and Mills, C. W., *From Max Weber*, Routledge and Kegan Paul, London 1948; Oxford University Press, New York 1946.

Hanson, N., *The Concept of the Positron*, Cambridge University Press, Cambridge 1963.

Hitchner, D. G. and Levine, C., *Comparative Government and Politics*, Harrap, London 1967.

Jacob, P. E. and Toscano, J. V. (eds.), *The Integration of Political Communities*, J. B. Lippincott, Philadelphia 1964.

Jenkins, T. P., *The Study of Political Theory*, Doubleday, New York 1955.

Kaplan, M. A., "The New Great Debate: Traditionalism versus Science in International Relations", *World Politics*, Vol. XIX, No. I, 1966.

Laslett, P. (ed.), *Philosophy, Politics and Society*, Blackwell, Oxford 1956.

Lasswell, H. D., *Collected Works*, Free Press, Glencoe, Ill. 1951.

——, *Psychopathology and Politics*, 1934, reprinted by Free Press, Glencoe, Ill. 1951.

Lasswell, H. D. and Kaplan, C., *Power and Society: A Framework for Political Inquiry*, Yale University, New Haven 1950.

Leontief, W., "The Structure of Development", *Scientific American*, September 1963.

Levy, M., *The Structure of Society*, Princeton University Press, Princeton, New Jersey 1952.

Lindberg, L., "The European Community as a Political System: Notes Toward the Construction of a Model", *Journal of Common Market Studies*, Vol. 5, 1967.

Lockwood, D., "Some Remarks on 'The Social System' ", *British Journal of Sociology*, Vol. 7, 1956.

Mackenzie, W. J. M., *Politics and Social Science*, Penguin, Harmondsworth 1967.

Malinowski, B., *Argonauts of the Western Pacific*, Routledge and Kegan Paul, London 1922; Dutton, New York 1922.

March, J. G., "An Introduction to the Theory and Measurement of Influence", *American Political Science Review*, Vol. 49, 1955.

March, J. G. (ed.), *Handbook of Organizations*, Rand McNally, Chicago 1965.

Martindale, D., "Sociological Theory and the Ideal Type" in L. Gross (ed.), *Symposium of Sociological Theory*, Harper and Row, London and New York 1959.

Marx, K., *Selected Works*, Foreign Languages Publishing House, Moscow 1958.

Merriam, C., *Political Power*, McGraw Hill, New York 1934.

Merton, R. K., *Social Theory and Social Structure*, Free Press, Glencoe, Ill. 1957.

Nettl, J. P., "The Concept of System in Political Science", *Political Studies*, October 1966.

Parsons, T., "Distribution of Power in American Society", *World Politics*, Vol. 10, October 1967.

——, "On the Concept of Influence", *Public Opinion Quarterly*, Vol. 24, 1963.

——, *The Social System*, Free Press, Glencoe, Ill. 1951.

Prior, A. N., *Formal Logic*, Oxford University Press, London 1955.

Radcliffe-Brown, A. R., *Andaman Islanders*, 1922, reprinted by Free Press, Glencoe, Ill. 1964.

——, *Structure and Function in Primitive Society*, Free Press, Glencoe, Ill. 1952.

Rappoport, A., "Various Meanings of Theory", *American Political Science Review*, Vol. LII, 1958.

Riggs, F. W., *Administration in Developing Countries: The Theory of Prismatic Society*, Houghton Mifflin, Boston.

Rostow, W. W., *The Stages of Economic Growth*, Cambridge University Press, Cambridge and New York 1960.

Runciman, W. G., *Social Science and Political Theory*, Cambridge University Press, 1963.

Russell, B., *Power: A New Social Analysis*, Allen and Unwin, London 1938; Barnes and Noble, New York 1962.

Russett, B., *Community and Contention: Britain and America in the Twentieth Century*, M.I.T. Press, Cambridge, Massachusetts 1963.

Sartori, G., "European Political Parties: The Case of Polarized Pluralism", in La Palombara, J. and Weiner, M. (eds.), *Political Parties and Political Development*, Princeton University Press, Princeton, New Jersey 1966.

Schumpeter, J. A., *Business Cycles*, McGraw-Hill, New York and London 1939.

————, *Capitalism, Socialism and Democracy*, Harper and Row, New York 1942.

————, "The Common Sense of Econometrics", *Econometrica*, Vol. I, 1933.

Singer, D., *Quantitative International Politics: Insights and Evidence*, Free Press, New York 1968.

Toulmin, S., *The Philosophy of Science*, Arrow Books, London 1962.

Truman, D. B., *The Governmental Process*, Knopf, New York 1951.

Van Dyke, V., *Political Science: A Philosophical Analysis*, Stevens, London 1960.

Wallas, G., *Human Nature in Politics*, Constable, London 1942; Peter Smith, Magnolia, Mass. 1962.

Weber, M., *The Theory of Social and Economic Organization*, trans. by A. M. Henderson and T. Parsons, Oxford University Press, London 1947.

Weiner, N., *Cybernetics, or Control and Communication in the Animal and the Machine*, New York 1948.

Weldon, T. D., *The Vocabulary of Politics*, Penguin, Harmondsworth 1953.

Wight, M., "Why Is There No International Theory", in Butterfield, H. and Wight, M. (eds.), *Diplomatic Investigations*, Allen and Unwin, London 1966.

Young, C., *Politics in the Congo: Decolonization and Independence*, Princeton University Press, Princeton, New Jersey 1965.

Zolberg, A., "A View from the Congo", *World Politics*, Vol. xix, 1966, pp. 137–57.

Index

DATE DUE

APR 15 '8	APR 6 '81		
DEC 10 '81			
DEC 10 '81	DEC 9 '81		
GAYLORD			PRINTED IN U.S.A.